A Father's Fight

Taking on
Alex Jones
and Reclaiming
the Truth About
Sandy Hook

Robbie Parker

DIVERSION
BOOKS

For Emilie, Madeline, and Samantha.
You are always worth fighting for.

—

Diversion Books
A division of Diversion Publishing Corp.
www.diversionbooks.com

For more information, email info@diversionbooks.com

Originally published in hardcover by Diversion Books, November 2024
First trade paperback edition, September 2025
Hardcover ISBN: 9781635769838
Trade Paperback ISBN: 9798895150856
e-ISBN: 9781635769753

Design by Neuwirth & Associates, Inc.
Cover design by Jonathan Sainsbury

Printed in the United States of America
1 3 5 7 9 10 8 6 4 2

Praise for *A Father's Fight*

"*A Father's Fight* is both a beautiful tribute to Robbie Parker's daughter Emilie and an invaluable lesson about the dangers of a post-truth era. Parker's tireless efforts in the name of justice are proof that, with enough courage and fierce determination, good triumphs over evil."

—KATIE COURIC, award-winning journalist and #1 *New York Times* bestselling author of *Going There*

"*A Father's Fight* is more than a compelling memoir, it's a deep dive into the evil forces that are dividing the country and the redemption of people who used their voices to win with the truth. Robbie Parker tells his story through the lens of a parent's love as he recounts not just the horrible events of the Sandy Hook School shooting and losing his beautiful daughter but the terror he faced with his family as that loss became a conspiracy theory. This book is a testament to a father's love, as well as an inside look at their fight for justice in the wake of unspeakable tragedy."

—LEE WOODRUFF, *New York Times* bestselling author of *In an Instant: A Family's Journey of Love and Healing*

"Robbie Parker's journey is every American dad's worst nightmare, squared. In the wake of his daughter's murder at Sandy Hook, he faced a decade of dollarized humiliation at the hands of Alex Jones and his army of conspiracy ghouls. In *A Father's Fight*, he leads us deep into the bizarre hell-dive, weaving a compellingly intimate and approachable narrative out of the years of unimaginable pain and abuse. . . . But then came more twists, the darkness thickened as Parker was forced to look within. A fearless and unique book."

—DAN REED, director of *The Truth vs. Alex Jones*

"Robbie Parker's story of fatherhood is one of walking humbly, loving tenderly, and—after losing his daughter at Sandy Hook—trying to grieve openly. His next mission, so powerfully portrayed in this book, was to confront evil by acting justly. Thus, the 'fight' in *A Father's Fight*, Parker's stirring account of his battle, on behalf of every parent and child, against weaponized lies."

—MARK K. SHRIVER, *New York Times* bestselling author and Christopher Award winner

"Robbie Parker went through the worst experience a parent can endure, and somehow, in the cloud of that all-consuming grief, found the courage to stand up to evil and help a community find justice. *A Father's Fight* details Robbie's courageous journey to reclaim his daughter's memory and protect his family against Alex Jones's intentional and directed campaign of hatred. His book is a heartbreaking encapsulation of grief and a stirring look at how community, love, and perseverance can take down a million-dollar propaganda machine. It's a devastating, inspirational, and empowering read."

—US SENATOR CHRIS MURPHY (D. Conn.)

"Mr. Parker takes an unimaginable experience and delivers a highly relatable story, equal parts tribute to his daughter and crash course on the importance of standing up to societal bullies. This book is a valuable insight into the damage that weaponized lying for profit does to real people."

—DAN FRIESEN, host of the *Knowledge Fight* podcast

"Robbie Parker courageously opens his soul to us in this emotional memoir related to the death of his daughter Emilie in the Sandy Hook Elementary School mass shooting. . . . This is a story about a father, unsure of himself at first, who fought back against a monstrous conspiracy theorist to honor the memory of his daughter. At times, I felt heartbroken while reading the book. Other times, I felt infuriated by a huckster's systematic harming of Robbie and the other Sandy Hook families so he could line his pockets with money from his cult followers. . . . But, more than anything, I felt proud that Robbie Parker had dug deep inside himself to justifiably take on an evil man."

—PETE SOUZA, former chief official White House photographer for President Obama

TABLE OF CONTENTS

PROLOGUE

"They Are Coming . . ."

SEPTEMBER 2022

Turning off Riverside Road at a secluded entrance in Sandy Hook, Connecticut, I was surrounded by beauty and deep meaning. Still, my body remembered the horrific tragedy that transpired here—and the continuing sinister incidents that have brought me back.

The crushed gravel path leading from the parking lot toward the Sandy Hook Memorial diverged into numerous paths. It meandered through and around natural landscaping, past a quote from President Obama etched in metal and set in stone. The terrain ascended and descended, subtly in some areas and sharply in others.

"The designers purposefully wanted to demonstrate what grief feels like," our guide and fellow surviving parent, Tricia Pinto, explained to my wife, Alissa, and me as we paused for a moment to take in the scenery. Alissa let go of my hand as the path narrowed, and I immediately missed her stabilizing comfort. I hung back while she moved forward a few paces until she looked back at me, her blue eyes moist. "Wow," she mouthed.

"All the paths lead away from and toward everything else. You'll notice they rise and fall," Tricia said.

That perfectly summarizes what grief feels like, I thought, as I took in the different twisting and intersecting paths. I remembered the first moment grief came to me, the night Emilie died, and ripped a piece of my heart out that has never been returned. Then, how our small town's communal grief spread out across the world, inspiring acts of love and compassion in a way I had never felt before and have yet to see since. I again felt the nagging doubt and question: What kind of husband and father would I be if my daughter had not been killed, compared to the one I became because she was?

As we moved along, I reset myself, checking in with every sense I possessed. My mouth tasted dry and metallic. With a deep breath, I smelled mulch around the plants hanging on to life despite the chill of this early fall afternoon. The water from a nearby creek trickled by softly. Fine gravel crunched under my feet, keeping me grounded even as the breeze ruffled my clothing and the sun's rays warmed my skin. I saw wildflowers with aging petals clinging onto stems alongside the path, but purposefully tried to avoid looking directly at the memorial. Still, I couldn't help but notice its simplistic beauty.

While walking, I kept reminding myself to breathe. On certain moments when I feel Emilie's presence or absence strongly, the air around me evaporates, leaving a vacuum. I often imagine this sensation will get easier with time, but it does not.

This monument had been almost ten years in the making. It filled me with apprehension, a tinge of anticipation, and another emotion I couldn't describe. Just through the trees behind us, up a small hill and out of sight from where I was standing, I heard children playing. It was the new Sandy Hook Elementary School. It sat intimately close—but not on the land for the memorial. Joyous cheers from recess transcended the distance. Excited screams and laughter pierced my body . . . but calmed my soul. The feeling, I realized, was longing.

Children being children, living so carefree, might seem a complete contradiction to the purpose of a memorial site. There we were, remembering the lives of twenty-six people—twenty of them children, including my daughter Emilie—all murdered inside their school. Yet the sound of infectious glee gave me exactly what I hoped this memorial would provide, a physical place to remember and feel those lives that were lived. To reminisce about who they were and what they meant to us, making them something more than just the story of how they perished. Those rambunctious voices brought precious memories of my daughter's laughter into the area inside my chest where grief resided.

The wandering paths finally led us to the memorial site. A magnificently humble structure, whose simple appearance only exemplified its breathtaking beauty. Granite stonework encircled a large but shallow pool of water flowing in a gentle circle. But it was the young sycamore tree that struck me with awe. Planted on a small island built in the center of the pool, the sycamore is renowned for its strength and perseverance. Along the massive perimeter of the water, the name of every life lived and taken was raised up and etched in perfect symmetry on twenty-six capstones. Twenty-six lives.

The three of us walked counterclockwise around the structure until we were in front of our oldest daughter's name:

Emilie Parker.

Seeing her name, her life, memorialized this way was humbling and painful. How can something so simple elicit so much?

A bell chimed and the children's chorus swelled before the tidal wave of sound rolled back into the school. "The flow of water," Tricia explained reverently, "completes a full circle. If we lay a flower inside, it will leave but then circles back around, symbolizing that what we lose can return."

My wife and I stared at our oldest daughter's name. I grabbed Alissa's hand but swore I could feel Emilie's gentle touch. The sound of her sweet voice lingered briefly in my mind . . . like the last note of a rousing symphony before everything goes silent. It's the silence that gets to me.

I peered through the thick trees past the new school to where the original Sandy Hook building once stood. That place where a twenty-year-old someone armed with more firepower than a soldier in battle carried out a brutal and unfathomable act against six- and seven-year-old children and their caring educators—simply because he wanted to.

When I looked over to my right at the firehouse where family members were told to wait for our children on that horrific day, I paused to feel the anger. I do not resist the searing pain and sorrow as I would have before. Grief has taught me to stop fearing these emotions and to allow them to flow through me, much like the nearby stream. But on that day in the firehouse, I only understood that this event was the absolute worst thing that could ever happen to my family. On that day, I recognized evil.

What I didn't know was that while Alissa and I and other parents anxiously awaited news, the voice of a different kind of evil seized upon that moment to do his worst. From his *Infowars* studio in Austin, Texas, the notorious conspiracy theorist Alex Jones claimed the Sandy Hook Elementary School shooting was *fake*, that it was staged, that it wasn't real—simply because he wanted to.

"Don't ever think this couldn't be staged," he warned with his laryngitic growl. "I told you they are going to come for our guns, look for mass shootings, and then magically it happens. They are coming. They are coming. They are coming!"

He deliberately stoked the fears of his rabid, loyal listeners while laying the foundation for who to blame—and who to fight—in order to "protect" their freedom to bear arms. This was a fight many of his listeners took seriously after Jones yelled into his microphone, "They are declaring war on the Second Amendment, period!"

Similar messages and warnings echoed throughout degenerate areas of the internet for days and weeks after the shooting. While in the physical world, an overwhelming amount of love and support from all around the globe descended on Newtown—and we felt it. We received an emotional letter from the president of Portugal telling me how touched he was when he learned I had been teaching Emilie to speak Portuguese. One afternoon we opened a package from a seventeen-year-old artist who sent a breathtaking charcoal drawing of Emilie, who had dreams of becoming an artist herself someday. I stared at this stunning portrait, mesmerized by how well it captured Emilie's eyes and vibrant spirit. The very personal and touching letter that accompanied the beautiful drawing described how she felt Emilie touched her life. "I'd like to think this drawing is from Emilie and me," she wrote, then explained that the drawing helped her realize that "my passion is for art; it is what I was meant to do." Complete strangers, friends, and acquaintances from long ago, even my elementary school librarian, found personal ways to express their sorrow and support for all the victims and their families.

How disorienting and confusing everything felt in those first days and weeks. We were weighed down by suffocating grief, while people across the world fought to lift us up with their kindness. In those raw moments, when I felt the pain of Emilie's loss, that loving support kept me afloat. In those first hours and days there was no way for me or Alissa to know what would lie ahead, though we already sensed we would need time to heal and that the love, compassion, and support we'd already experienced would be a vital lifeline. We knew that every new day was another day between us and the last day we shared with Emilie, so we wanted to cherish those precious moments, as painful as they were. All Alissa and I wanted to do was grieve. With two surviving daughters to care for, we understood that to protect our family, ourselves, and our marriage, we needed to learn how to deal with grief. We felt that understanding and learning from grief needed to be our number one priority. Without knowing anything yet, we somehow knew that this was our family's key to survival—how Emilie's memory would live on.

YET, FOR US, and for me personally, there existed another constant, powerful, and dangerous force exerting itself on our already complicated grieving process. On the very day of the shooting, Alex Jones gave no thought toward grief but instead declared war on those immersed in it. And his minions were prepared to fight and wasted no time heeding the call. They attacked.

"Fucking liar, your daughter ain't dead!" one commented on Emilie's memorial page that friends of ours started on Facebook.

"Viva 2nd Amendment! Try and take my guns, but watch your back, because we are coming for you!" said another, this one linked with an *Infowars* article and video showing Alex Jones.

On that fateful day, Emilie and her friends experienced evil. Alex Jones spoke evil. In the months and years afterward, we have felt the aftershocks from both. From the day the shooter entered Sandy Hook Elementary to the very afternoon we visited the memorial, we were under a concentrated and relentless attack.

GRIEF REQUIRES A CONSTANT EXERTION of energy, time, and focus. This time immediately after Emilie's death felt sacrosanct, a time for our family to be focused on each other. We lost someone so precious to all of us. I wanted to hold everyone tight, protect them, and somehow let them know everything would be okay. However, because of conspiracy theorists, I was forced to direct my focus away from my family's grief. I was disoriented and hurt by what I was seeing, and spent priceless hours trying to purge these hateful attacks from the internet and reporting them to social media companies. This distraction siphoned energy and stole precious moments—moments that should have been sacred.

One morning, two days before Emilie's funeral, I received a disturbing personal message online. The anonymous author articulated in exquisite detail the physical harm I could expect if he ever saw me in person. After having just lost a daughter, I became hypervigilant with my responsibility to protect my family. Instead of being open to my wife's and daughter's emotional needs, as grief demands, I found myself being guarded. When out in public together, I wasn't present but felt vulnerable and hyperfocused on everything around us. Like we were timid game animals grazing in the meadow, always alert and ready to give the signal to run.

I could not fight back with the intensity required to mount the defense needed to keep my family protected. Every time I sacrificed time and energy to combat this war, there was a direct, negative impact on my family—and equally heart-wrenching, to my ability to grieve my own daughter properly. My hypervigilance made me feel less connected to my family, to Emilie, and to myself.

Despite all my efforts to protect my family, show up in grief, be an example to my two living children, to deeply honor Emilie's life and memory, I felt that I was failing—and I was. No matter what, the attacks just kept coming, leaving me feeling despondent, bitter, and angry. Alissa worried how this was affecting me and tenderly tried to help me become more present and balanced in our desires to be safe and grieve. But I was too entrenched to hear what she was saying. Instead, I continued to engage in an insurmountable battle against a multimillion-dollar propaganda machine fueled by hate and lies. The longer I remained connected to this fight alone, the more it disconnected me from my own voice, my own self, and eventually my own power.

EVEN AS I STOOD DIRECTLY in front of Emilie's name at the memorial a decade later, all I could hear in my mind was Alex Jones's voice: "And here is Robbie Parker, a 'supposed' father of one of the victims . . ." Alissa grabbed my hand, which paused the voice long enough for me to reel myself back into the present moment. My body had become tense and rigid. The pain was familiar and present as if December 14, 2012, were only a few days ago.

I took another deep breath, smelled the mulch again, and tuned into the rustling autumn breeze. Finally, I bent over to touch the circular water flowing within the memorial's structure. We took another turn through the memorial site, along a different path than the one that led us to Emilie's name. I was glad we came, but I hated that it had to be here at all.

We looked around and found Tricia with her head bowed in a solemn appearance that Alissa and I recognized immediately. Her eyes were moist when we approached her, in front of her son's name, *Jack Pinto*, etched in stone. We all hugged each other with a type of embrace that only we can provide for one another.

Back in the car, Alissa and I sat quietly, allowing our bodies to absorb the emotions from that experience. Alissa finally spoke, her tone solemn: "I can't believe it's been almost ten years."

"I know," I rasped, clearing the frog from my throat. "It's hard to fathom everything we've been through."

She placed a hand on my cheek, the way married couples do when they have so much to say but not any of the words to say them. But she managed. "You've got this."

With those three words, she brought us both back to the present moment and why we were there, in Connecticut, after having left nine years prior to give our family a fresh start. We were there, alongside fourteen other Sandy Hook family members and victims, to hold Alex Jones accountable for the insurmountable pain and suffering he caused innocent people. I was there to fight the war I never wanted to fight. For nearly a decade, I'd made myself small. I told my friends and my family that the vitriolic hate, the terrifying threats, and the online slander that defiled Emilie's name and memory didn't affect me. I believed that if I ignored the bully that is Alex Jones long enough he would eventually move on. It was a self-defeating battle that left me without my voice, without my power. I was back in Connecticut to finally restore and reclaim what was taken after the shooting. Finally, after years of litigation, appeals, depositions, and utilizing every strategy to avoid accountability, alt-right conspiracy theorist and snake oil peddler Alex Jones would stand trial. Lingering in the pit of my stomach, for me, for my wife, and for all of us lay the burning question: *Will Alex Jones have the courage to show up and face us?*

Because I was here to take him on face-to-face in court and stand against those who felt emboldened and entitled to attack grieving families of murdered children. Because as grief taught us and the memorial pool symbolized, what we lose will come back to us *if* we fight for it.

This story isn't just mine to share. It's for all of us because we have all lived through these tumultuous times together, in our own ways and along our own paths. As you read this story, I hope that our wandering paths intersect many times, proving how connected we are with one another. These connections can happen, regardless of where we were born, who we vote for, where our news comes from, or what teams we support.

Grief has taught me that.

So, as we continue to share our human experiences together, may we do so with greater compassion and empathy for one another.

The only way the mirage of our differences disappears is when we see each other clearly. It's time we start new conversations that move us forward, forging relationships that bring us together. Which becomes impossible when lies are purposefully used to separate me from you and us from them. Only the truth, the real truth, will set us free and initiate the kind of healing we all so desperately need.

A Father's Fight

Chapter 1
That Day

Alissa and I said very little as we approached all-too-familiar parts of Connecticut. Once an area filled with precious, sweet memories, it was now imbued with painful and emotional triggers.

Like the wooded landscape outside the car that was transitioning from one season into another, we'd been forced to accept continuous change, often without any control or say in the matter. Off in the distance we spotted Danbury Hospital, where I began working in early 2012. Farther north out of sight was the small house we rented on Candlewood Lake after first moving to the area. That was where my oldest daughter of three, Emilie Parker, first attended kindergarten at Consolidated Elementary School before we settled in Sandy Hook. With eclectic outfits of her own choosing, piercing blue eyes, and an ever-talkative, sociable personality, she was immediately welcomed by teachers and classmates alike. After her first week she came home and announced she met her soulmate and future husband, Parker.

"Can you believe it, Mom?" Emilie asked, smiling after school one afternoon. "If we got married, his name could be Parker Parker!"

She burst out laughing, handing Alissa a drawing she and Parker had sketched of the house they would live in one day.

As we passed the exit where the old Sandy Hook Elementary School sat out of sight among the trees, my throat burned as I recalled one of my fondest memories. Emilie was clutching a thrift store frame she had repainted herself that encompassed her first-grade class picture. She followed Alissa all over the house chattering about every one of her classmates, each one her friend.

"This is Charlotte Bacon—isn't that funny, Mom?" she asked, beaming. "Her last name is Bacon, like bakin' a cake!" Emilie giggled, and so did Alissa as our daughter gushed on. "And this is James Mattioli and Jessica Rekos and Grace McDonnell and Joey—Mom, look! This is Joey." Joey, or Josephine Gay, was autistic and non-verbal. The chatty Emilie and the non-verbal Joey were a fantastic pair and best friends. "Then there's Olivia, Noah, Daniel, Caroline, Benjamin, Allison . . ." Emilie loved her classmates and her school. And that's where she died with them.

Like Emilie, I felt a deep sense of love for the parents of her classmates who were also killed. Though in reality, I didn't know the other families very well. We moved to Newtown just eight months before the shooting and quickly became immersed in remodeling our home. It felt like the only people I recognized in town, outside of work and church, were Home Depot employees.

That spring of 2012, Alissa's father had qualified for the Boston Marathon. He was also very helpful with remodels, a skill he had picked up helping his dad build houses when he was younger. So these were the perfect excuses for my in-laws' first visit to our new home. After a week of remodeling and chores, we set out for Boston to watch "Grandpa" run in the Boston Marathon, checking off a long-standing bucket list item for him. Emilie, Madeline, and Samantha proudly displayed their homemade signs, jumping and cheering every time their grandpa passed by.

At the same time, my favorite baseball team, the Texas Rangers, were playing in Boston. Alissa's family loved going to baseball games, so I also got to check off a bucket list item: attending a Rangers game at historic Fenway Park. This trip was so special for everyone because, as it turned out, it was the last time all of us were together. Five months later, in September 2012, Alissa's father was involved in a horrible bicycling accident while riding in a one-day, 210-mile race from Logan, Utah, to Jackson Hole, Wyoming. We spent a month flying back and forth to Utah and were all present when he passed three weeks later. Between the move, the remodel, and Alissa's father's passing, we had inadvertently isolated ourselves from the greater Newtown community.

But after December 14, a strong kinship grew between us and the other parents. They were the only people on Earth in the *you just get it* group. Our group, known throughout town as *The Families,* met regularly for meetings with the state police and FBI when they provided updates into their investigations. We came together at times to help with yardwork or to provide our voices in areas that mattered to us. Such as battling the United Way after they raised tens of millions of dollars to support Newtown families, while actually putting that money into their general fund. Together we rooted for and supported the many non-profit organizations some of the families started to honor their children or evoke change in the world. Every once in a while I would receive texts from a few other dads wanting to go out for drinks after a particularly hard day.

But for a long time, I held the other parents at arm's length. I had always felt some level of angst when I was around other Sandy Hook parents, due to the shame I carried all these years for my role in what became the Sandy Hook conspiracy movement. In my mind, I was to blame for it ever becoming a movement at all. None of the other families ever said or did anything to confirm this assumption, but I was convinced they believed this was all my fault. After all, it was my idea to hold a press conference that would become the fodder Alex Jones used to spew the lies that fueled hatred and slander toward all the Sandy Hook families. I bore the blame as a form of penance for the ruthless assault we suffered due to my carelessness. Because we moved out of Newtown a year after the shooting, I had only seen some of my fellow plaintiffs once since we left, and that was a lawsuit-related issue; the others I hadn't seen at all. Still, because of what we had experienced together on the levels we did connect, they were closer than family for me. I cared about them, and the notion that I had let them down fueled my guilt and personal insecurities that whole night and into the first day of the trial.

Could this trial somehow ease that burden? Or would it only serve to exacerbate those feelings and beliefs? I did not know, but at this point there was only one way to find out.

THE FIRST DAY OF TRIAL had arrived and everyone met in the hotel lobby before walking to the courthouse together. When the elevator doors opened, there in the foyer stood Jennifer Hensel. My heart leaped seeing her again. Her eyes, so dark and warm like her daughter Avielle's had been, met mine as we exited the elevator.

"Alissa . . . Robbie," she said, almost surprised. "It's so good to see you."

"It is so good to see you," I said with some relief. I glanced around the lobby and saw other families arriving. Mark and Jackie Bardon's son Daniel was killed in the same classroom as Emilie. The Bardons are a musical family, each able to play multiple instruments, and Daniel had a propensity for the drums. I saw David and Francine Wheeler, whose son Benjamin died alongside Emilie and Daniel. I first met them at a meeting with other families shortly after the shooting. David was pleasant and talkative when he introduced himself to me at a time when I was neither of those things. I liked them very much, but did not know them well.

I was excited to see Nicole and Ian Hockley arrive. Ian was the first parent I met after the shooting, and I have felt the seedlings of a proper friendship in our interactions over the years—if only those seeds had fallen on less-traumatic soil. Their son Dylan was autistic and died in the protective arms of his special needs aide, Anne Marie Murphy. Nicole threw herself into advocacy work spending countless hours promoting programs involving gun, school, and community safety.

The other plaintiffs were family members of adult victims from the shooting. Bill Sherlock, a dapper and delightful gentleman whose wife, Mary, was the school psychologist. Bill always made me feel comfortable in these group settings, even when I wasn't. Victoria Soto was a first-grade teacher who died protecting her students. I was happy to meet her mother, Donna, and siblings, Carlee, Jillian, and Matthew. Dawn Hochsprung, the school principal, was the first person to encounter the shooter. Her daughter Erica Lafferty pushed hard for the lawsuit against Alex Jones to be filed.

As greetings and hugs abounded in that hotel lobby, I was filled with a sense of fellowship that can only be felt among these people. Today meant so much to all of us after the long journey we experienced just to reach the trial. But this gathering of Sandy Hook families was different from any other I had been a part of before. What brought us together that morning, what we were fighting for this time, was not about what happened to our children, wife, or sister. We were there because of what happened directly to us because of Alex Jones. We were there to fight for ourselves and for each other.

A few minutes later all of us walked the half mile from that hotel lobby, past lines of cameras and reporters, and entered the courthouse together. The courtroom assigned for this case was larger than what I had envisioned with a high, twenty-foot ceiling. Yards of empty space separated the judge's bench, jury box, and the attorneys' tables. Anemic beige walls and pale carpet under light brown wooden structures and trim gave the room a homely vibe. The room was already packed except for a section on the first three rows reserved for plaintiffs and families. Together we listened to one of our attorneys during his opening statement as he turned to the jury, his eyes pleading. "We need you to understand the truth of what happened that day."

I held Alissa's hand and looked around the courtroom, making eye contact with Erica Lafferty, Nicole Hockley, and Francine Wheeler. Because, without a word, we knew "that day" is what tore us apart individually and brought us together collectively. Almost everyone has their own "that day" experience—an event that somehow demarcates one's life into the chronology of *before* that day and what happened after it.

THAT DAY, FRIDAY, DECEMBER 14, 2012, I awoke early for work and felt the excitement that had been building in our house all week. Emilie, after hearing the story about the real St. Nicholas, took it upon herself to start a family toy drive. After rummaging in the garage, she found what she called "the perfect box" and walked through the living room, right past the Christmas tree, nativity advent calendar, and her mother on the couch before disappearing into her room. Emilie was always full of ideas and fanciful plans, so her actions were no surprise to Alissa, who followed her with a quizzical stare. "Mom, I'm collecting toys to donate for other kids," she announced when she reappeared a little while later holding up the box for Alissa to see her miscellaneous collection of toys, stuffed animals, dolls, and doll clothes. "But I don't have enough." With a grin, she raced to recruit her two younger sisters, Madeline and Samantha. Her spirit of philanthropy was not as easily adopted by her sisters when she asked them to donate their precious toys to join hers inside the box, but Emilie pressed forward and with some older sisterly love, persuasion, and bartering, everyone eventually was on board. Soon, the box was full to the brim. But before it could be considered complete, Emilie rushed to grab something from her room, then rejoined everyone in Samantha's room.

"There," she said, placing a piece of her artwork into the box. It was as though she knew that only by giving away something truly meaningful would it be meaningful for someone else. With that, the donation box was ready.

To kick off the Christmas break, Alissa and I agreed at the end of the week, we would all drop the box off at Make a Home Foundation, a local non-profit. We visited this store often during our remodel to pick out old furniture we could refurbish on our tight budget. Emilie loved that store because she "negotiated" with the owners to keep random or broken items she found lying around. These special items were always reused in Emilie's many artistic projects.

Emilie was a notoriously early riser. So much so that we taught her how to tell time just so we could make a rule that she was not allowed to come to our room before 7:00 a.m. After I woke up that Friday morning full of anticipation, I cracked Emilie's door at six forty-five and, of course, she was already awake, sitting obediently on the edge of her bed waiting. She saw me, looked at her clock, then back to me, and smiled.

"Bom dia!" she exclaimed excitedly in Portuguese. I had lived in Brazil for two years after high school, becoming fluent in the language. Recently I had started teaching Emilie.

"Bom dia você," I replied back. "E cómo está?" *Good morning to you and how is it going?*

"Estou bem." *I am good*, she answered, still smiling.

"Está bem; eu te amo." *That's good; I love you.*

"Eu te amo." *I love you.*

"I know it is before seven, but Mom is awake so you can go ahead and snuggle with her if you want." After a hug, Emilie skipped off to Alissa, because Emilie never simply walked anywhere.

By the time I was ready to leave for work, the whole house was awake with everyone in Samantha's room elated that today the box, still nestled along the wall, would be donated for other children in need. After quick hugs and kisses for everyone, I was out the door. A short while later, Alissa and the girls walked to the end of our road to meet Emilie's school bus. Like every other morning. Alissa chatted with our neighbors while the kids ran around. When the school-aged children had to leave, Emilie pranced over to the opened doors, bounded up onto the bus, and headed off for school. By the time the bus dropped Emilie off at Sandy Hook Elementary, I was already busy at the hospital.

I WAS STILL NEW TO DANBURY HOSPITAL, having worked there for just shy of a year, but had quickly been accepted and woven into our unit's fabric. As a physician assistant in the neonatal intensive care unit I spend my mornings poring over recent lab results, performing physical exams, and talking with staff about each baby prior to starting our patient rounds. The NICU can be a chaotic, thrilling, exhausting, and at times tragic place to work. It is also the most special place in any hospital with the best patients anyone could care for—and I love it. That morning, during our patient rounds, I received a disturbing voicemail.

> Hello, this is Pat Llodra, Newtown First Selectman, calling to inform you that all Newtown public schools have been placed in lockdown due to a reported shooting at one of our schools.

Before I even attempted to comprehend what I just heard, my phone rang again. This time it was Alissa asking if I'd received the call about the lockdown.

"What do you think is going on?" she asked. "What should I do?"

"I have no clue," I stammered, searching for the right thing to say. "This has got to be something at the high school, right? I mean that's where something like a shooting would happen."

"What if it isn't at the high school?" Alissa asked, concerned. "Emilie's classroom is in that front hallway."

I had no answer. Alissa, not one to wait for instructions, went to pick up Madeline from preschool. When I turned on the TV in the break room a reporter announced that a shooting had been reported at Sandy Hook Elementary School in Newtown, Connecticut. She read the teleprompter dispassionately as if the words entered her eyes and escaped her lips without giving her mind a chance to process what she was saying. My heart plummeted.

"Hey," I said anxiously when I called Alissa back. "The shooting was at Sandy Hook."

"I know," Alissa broke in, breathless. "The other parents at the preschool told me. I'm going there now. I'll update you when I get there. Okay?"

"Okay," I responded helplessly, knowing there wasn't anything else I could do. "I love you," I added, trying to sound brave and reassuring.

"Love you," she said.

News of the shooting spread fast as the hospital went into lockdown in preparation for a community disaster. All entrances had been blocked; nobody was allowed to enter or leave. Hospital security and local police officers were present and visible to maintain order. The emergency department was preparing for an influx of trauma patients, and other hospital staff were on high alert. The lockdown did not affect the NICU directly, but some of our babies' parents were not allowed inside the hospital.

The mood in the unit became heavy, filling up with anticipation. A NICU nurse ran up to me and said her husband was a firefighter and told her the shooting was at Sandy Hook.

"Is Emilie okay?" she asked. Other nurses and the neonatologist gathered around. I forced myself to stay composed and told them Alissa was on her way to the school right now. Then I turned around quickly because the pressure building in my chest felt stronger with everyone looking at me. With nowhere to go or anything to do, the tension built while we did the only thing we could do—wait.

Truthfully, I had no intuition about what I *should* be feeling or what I *should* be thinking. I only felt antsy, as a micro-popping sensation prickled all over my body, just under my skin. Here I was, at a hospital where I work helping other families' children during a crisis. Now I was unsure how to handle a crisis that involved my child, my family and not someone else's. After what felt like hours, Alissa called back.

"What's going on?" I asked, more tersely than I really wanted.

"It's crazy here. There are so many people and it's just chaos. I let the girls go home with the Carsons, while I look for Emilie—" Alissa paused for a second. "Hold on. Let me call you back in a minute."

I tried to be patient but I just couldn't wait around any longer. If the Carsons, our neighbors down the street, left with my daughters, then I needed to be with them or with Alissa, but not at the hospital anymore.

And I wasn't the only one who felt that way. I found the neonatologist and we both proclaimed, "I need to go," "You need to go," in unison. I rushed to my call room, changed out of my hospital scrubs and into my street clothes. Running down a back stairwell, I remembered that we were still in lockdown and I couldn't leave, but I kept running. I didn't care; surely someone would understand. It had been hours at this point and Emilie still was not accounted for. Of course they would let me go be with my wife and children.

The door at the bottom of the stairwell opened up to a crowded waiting area right outside of the emergency room. I worked my way through the crowd toward a door when a police officer stopped me, asking where I was going. I showed him my hospital badge and explained that my daughter went to Sandy Hook, and my wife hadn't found her yet. The officer cut me off:

"How many kids go to that school?" he asked abruptly.

Confused and irritated by his question, I answered, "I have no clue. Four hundred?"

"Exactly. So what are the chances something happened to your daughter?"

I just stared back at him.

Then, in a tone only reserved for know-it-all, insecure older brothers, he said, "So why don't you go wait like everyone else until you get some real news." Had Alissa not called me at that moment, I might have started a mutiny.

"Do I need to go there?"

"No!" she said quickly. "I heard that some kids were injured and taken to the hospital. If Emilie is hurt, then you are right where she needs you to be. I just got sent into a conference room in that firehouse on the corner where they will start reuniting families. I'll stay here, you find out what you can, and we'll keep updating each other."

I hung up the phone, unsure what exactly I should do next, when I was hit with the realization of what was actually happening. There was a shooting at an elementary school. Children were injured, which meant children had been shot, and we didn't know if Emilie was one of them. If Emilie was at the hospital, no one was going to come looking for me. I would need to look for her myself. Across the waiting area, I noticed another door with a badge scanner next to it. I didn't know what to do, but I did have a badge, and I sensed my answer might lie on the other side of the door that led to a back entrance for the emergency department.

Once inside, I became nervous knowing I didn't belong there. Being in plain street clothes, I couldn't go around peeking behind curtains or opening patient doors. Instead, I kept my badge as visible as possible and walked around listening for anything that could help me figure out what to do next.

It took me a minute to realize that the atmosphere inside the emergency room was very different from the chaos in the waiting area, or the tension I felt in the NICU. The ER was eerily calm. There was nobody running around. No one was barking orders at nurses or residents. The lack of stress was seriously conflicting with everything I had felt the last few hours. Which made me feel uncomfortable sneaking and poking around, unable to camouflage myself in the chaos I expected. Then someone caught me.

"Robbie?"

I looked up and recognized an ER doctor down the corridor. Weeks earlier, a newborn had been found unresponsive at home and was brought by ambulance to the hospital. I was called to place a breathing tube and help this doctor with the resuscitation.

"What are you doing down here?" he said in a steady, compassionate voice. My emotions, I'm sure, were written all across my face.

"My daughter goes to Sandy Hook. My wife is at the firehouse waiting and hasn't heard anything about her yet. She asked me to find out if our daughter was one of the children that were brought here because if she *is* here"—my voice trailed off—"she needs me."

He looked at me for a moment, then gently took my arm and started leading me to the ambulance bay. "I think it is best if you go and be with your wife right now."

His words filled me with a sense of relief and foreboding. His response not only gave me permission to leave the hospital, but confirmed Emilie was not there. That meant one of two things, and my answers would not be found here.

Outside, I called Alissa. "I've done all I can; I don't think she's here," I told her. "I'm coming to you now."

"Yes, please come. It's crowded in here and they said a state police officer would give us an update soon." Her voice sounded uneasy.

"I'll be right there." I hung up and sped straight to Sandy Hook.

The narrow roads leading to the school in the small village of Sandy Hook were impenetrably clogged with cars. I parked behind a shop and sprinted the half mile toward Alissa in the firehouse, completely oblivious of the satellite news vans, the makeshift podium with an overabundance of microphones, past everyone in suits, uniforms, and cameras. But when I barged into the conference room, it was like I ran into a brick wall. The room was heavy, similar to the pressure one feels as they descend deep underwater. Alissa stood up, waving me over. She quickly filled me in on some details, her face filled with anguish. She told me it was confirmed twenty children had been killed. An officer told them no details or names would be shared until they'd accounted for everyone.

"They are still searching for other children," she said. "The officer said he would come back later with another update." Then her eyes found mine as if she was trying to bring me into her "mom" place. That special place just outside of a mother's consciousness where the love and feelings about their children are so strong, it would be impossible to keep them consciously present at all times. She wanted to share her worries and help me feel what she was feeling. Then she whispered, "Robbie," quietly so no one else could hear. "Is she dead?" "Of course not," I said and held her in my arms as tight as I could, somehow convinced that the more conviction I put in my answer, the more I could ward off the fear and doubt permeating the suffocating conference room.

It was a noble but futile effort. The question *Is she dead?* lingered between us without a definitive answer to the contrary. Just speaking the question into existence seemed to release every emotion Alissa had been holding in so tightly for hours in order to function. Her breathing started to become faster and more shallow, her face grew pale, and her body even more limp.

A paramedic noticed and responded quickly with an oxygen mask. Alissa was starting to have a panic attack. I held her face in my hands. "Look at me. Take a deep breath," I said calmly. Her eyes remained fixed on mine while the paramedic checked her vitals. "Alissa, just keep breathing, nice and slow." I continued, "If we can't get your oxygen levels up, I'm afraid they may want to take you away. I'm here now. I'm with you. I need you." Alissa's eyes changed focus again with a sense of determination. The color returned to her face. She took the mask off, handed it to the paramedics, and she got back into the chair next to me. "I'm not going anywhere," she said.

For hours, the only update we received from the state police was that there were no updates to give. The lack of information, along with the amount of time ticking away, compounded the tension and stress in the room. One officer approached Alissa and me asking for a description of our daughter. He jotted down the details of her blonde hair, blue eyes, white-and-pink ruffled skirt in his clichéd pocket notebook. We gave him our phone numbers and then he left. I looked around and noticed that any spark of hope that may have been in the faces of the parents when they entered that conference room had diminished to a small, delicate flicker. Still, it felt as if everyone was grasping to hold on to the last bit of its glow. We sat and waited.

Word of the shooting spread faster across the country than time was passing inside the firehouse. We were inundated with text messages from loved ones in Utah, New Mexico, and Oregon, lovingly asking if Emilie was okay. With no information to share, we didn't know what to say. Eventually, we stopped responding.

During those exact moments, Alex Emerick Jones, a man I never knew existed, heard about the shooting. He recognized it as an opportunity and pounced. While Alissa and I held hands, hope slipping between our interlocked fingers, Alex Jones went live.

"Connecticut school massacre looks like false flag, witnesses say." He broadcasted a lie made up out of thin air to his millions of listeners. Neither Alex Jones nor any of his staff ever spoke to anyone in Connecticut that day. It was a lie told because he knew his audience would believe him over anyone and anything else. And he used that misplaced trust for everything it was worth.

By 2012, Alex Jones had become a well-known figure in the alt-right, fringe conspiracy community. His conspiratorial nature and temper dated back to high school in the North Texas town of Rockwall, where he was known as a bully and a tyrant. Jones himself has told an outlandish story of being assaulted by local police after he accused the officers presenting at an anti-drug school assembly of selling cocaine at teen pool parties. No one has ever been able to corroborate that story. However, other stories about him from that time are verifiably true. Jones once beat a classmate, named Jared, so profoundly that he was hospitalized with a fractured skull and broken facial bones. David Jones, Alex's father and a wealthy dentist, quickly saved his son from accountability and assault charges by paying off the victim's family—then relocated his family from North Texas to Austin.

In the '90s, Alex Jones's gift of gab and ability to spin tales earned him a radio show, which he produced and broadcasted from his child's bedroom. Before being given airtime on Austin Community Access, his show was like a Weird Al version of current events, if you replaced wacky and satirical jokes with fearmongering and outlandish conspiracies. Instead of changing lyrics, Jones twisted the truth of official reports from local and national news. He manipulated them to fit his own distrusting worldview of radical government and elites. For many listeners, he was nothing more than an entertaining quack. But slowly, the showmanship of his alternate reality garnered popularity and a cultlike following.

After the historic and tragic Waco standoff against the Branch Davidians in 1993, he railed against the government and reported facts to spread his own theories about world domination and the deep state. Globalists, as he called them, were a secret group of elites aimed at stripping rights away from citizens in the form of mind control, to eventually enslave everyone into one tyrannical world government.

Jones's shrewd use of the early internet in the '90s and social media in the 2000s earned him more clout over the years. His messages eventually reached millions of listeners over hundreds of syndicated radio stations in the country. By tapping into his listeners' fears of being overlooked and mistreated by the government, he became a voice of "reason and truth" to them—a voice they were emphatically encouraged to follow while being warned to distrust many other sources of information. By 2012, he was maturing out of fringe alt-right obscurity, inching ever closer to the mainstream while his revenue growth followed suit.

When other people heard about the massacre of six-year-old children at Sandy Hook and those who cared for them, they wept. When Alex Jones heard the same news, he salivated. The black powder of fear he had been stoking for years was primed for ignition. With the Sandy Hook shooting, he found the perfect match.

"Don't ever think this couldn't be staged!" he growled into the microphone, gaslighting any logical thought his loyal listeners may have had. Jones used the slaughter of innocent children to tap into a primal fear shared by millions of Americans that their Second Amendment rights were being threatened.

"I told you, they are coming for our guns; look for mass shootings, and then magically it happens," Jones prophesied, verbally striking the illusory match. Then he ignited the carefully arranged fuse with this dire premonition: "They are coming. They are coming. They are coming."

After providing descriptions of Emilie's appearance and her clothes to police officers, who had still not given any of us an update, Governor Dannel Malloy, flanked by an entourage, entered the conference room, which was by now packed with a miscellaneous collection of first responders, social workers, and clergy from every denomination (with a surprisingly large presence of nuns). They were all there to help but, in my mind, mainly added emotional energy to a room that was desperate for a release valve.

In those long hours of waiting, we didn't see a single family reunification. One nun approached us, uninvited, and started asking me and Alissa some fairly insensitive questions. "Did you have a boy or a girl? How old was she? What was her name?" We were uncomfortable with her questions and thankfully someone came and ushered the nun away. However, due to the nature of her questions, we were left wondering if she somehow knew more information than we did. Again, we had not received any news after the first announcement over four hours earlier, and her questions, though well-intended, were very hurtful.

So, by the time the governor arrived, my adrenaline rush had diminished. I was emotionally taxed and now confused about why the governor was addressing all of us in a manner that suggested that *none* of our children had survived. One mother interrupted him, "So are you trying to tell us that all of our kids are dead?"

The governor looked stunned, as though someone had forgotten to remind him that we had not yet received any updates. The answer stumbled out of his mouth: "Yes." Then he paused, trying to find the right words in an impossible situation.

Alissa spoke up, quick to grasp onto hope. "What about the children that went to the hospital? What is their status?"

Again, like a deer in the headlights, the governor answered, "They have expired."

Expired. In that instant, any remaining flicker of hope evaporated, leaving an emotional vacuum in its place.

The room quickly began spinning, transporting us into some alternate reality where time, thought, and emotions no longer had any meaning. My wife and I glanced at each other, saw a door in the back corner of the conference room, and bolted for it. Outside, in the long shadows of the firehouse, we found some space to ourselves, where we could stand and hold on to each other. It was surreal.

"I want to go home," Alissa said. "There is nothing for me here."

I looked into her eyes and nodded and took her hand. We walked toward my car, but as we rounded the corner of the firehouse, we collided with a swarm of photographers. *Click! Click click click click . . .* It didn't end. If I had any sense of normalcy in the moment, I would have been appalled or outraged—but there was nothing normal about that moment. All I wanted to do was get home. I wrapped a protective arm around Alissa and kept walking until the photographers were forced to give way. Eventually a young fireman moved in front of us, waving his arms and ordering people to step back. He cleared a way for us through the pack of photographers until we at last had a path to our car. I mouthed a silent *thank you* to him and never looked back.

At home, we had the unspeakable task of explaining to Madeline and Samantha, aged four and three, that their sister Emilie had been killed—something I would never wish on another soul. Watching their sweet, innocent faces as they tried to understand what we were telling them left me feeling like a fraud. As parents we told our children we would never let anything hurt them, and we failed. I knew I couldn't make that promise ever again, but the need to keep my family safe expanded exponentially that evening. I reframed my promise, telling them I would do everything in my power to be their unshakable protector. Alissa and I then separated, taking our phones to different sides of the house while we began making phone call after phone call. Amid torrents of helpless sobs on both sides of the line, we were forced to repeat that Emilie was killed many times over as we broke the news to our respective family members. Everyone loved Emilie so much. She was a bright, bright light in our world, and none of us could stand the fact that her brilliance had been snuffed out. It was the most unbearable thing I'd ever experienced.

That evening we received a visit from our church's ecclesiastical leadership. They were so compassionate and loving, we felt them beside us as they promised to return the following day to begin planning the logistical steps for the upcoming funeral. Before they left, the three men warned us not to venture outside due to the large police and media presence in town.

It wasn't long after they left when my phone rang. I was completely spent. I had no desire to talk to anyone. I couldn't bear the thought of sharing the news again and listening to more cries. But the name on the screen was one of my closest childhood friends, Brad. I summoned any remaining composure I had and answered his call only to find out it wasn't just Brad calling, but our good friend Alan along with both of their wives, Camille and Brooke.

Strong emotions poured over the phone from everyone. "We're so sorry. We are here for you. We love you!"

All day long I had been containing emotions and keeping composure. I kept my emotions in check that morning, hiding my disappointment that I wouldn't be home in time to go to the donation center that afternoon. I was calm in the NICU after news of the shooting came out, reassuring everyone else that we would be okay. I didn't panic in the emergency room looking for my little girl. I never let go of hope in the firehouse, until it was taken away from all of us. And I didn't break during phone call after phone call to each one of my family members. I wanted to be the strong father Alissa and the girls could count on.

But hearing my two best buds express their love and heartbreak shook whatever composure I was still holding on to. Brad, Alan, and I have remained close since middle school. We stuck together through everything a set of friends could experience: love, heartbreak, thrills, scares, weddings, children, careers, and distance. We had never given up on each other, no matter what. And here they were once again.

"We don't want to bother you," Brad said, "but we wanted to help without overwhelming you." I sank deep into my couch, letting tears silently pour down my checks as they explained everything they had done after hearing Emilie was killed. They figured we would want to bury Emilie back in Utah and didn't want us worrying about the cost. So Brooke started a memorial page on Facebook, while Brad's little brother opened an account at the credit union he worked for. "We figured enough of our high school friends may want to donate some money to at least help cover the expenses to bring Emilie home."

I broke. All composure gone. "That sounds amazing; thank you," I managed between sobs. "I love you guys."

"We love you all," rang four voices in unison. I couldn't stop crying even after I hung up. Their kindness broke me open. While I was busy being strong, they saw I needed love. I let Alissa know what they had done for us, and she was equally astounded and moved.

It wasn't long after my call with Brad and Alan ended that my phone rang again. I didn't recognize the number, but thought it could be the police officer who said he would be in touch, so I answered.

"Hello, my name is Steve. I'm a reporter from—"

Shocked, I hung up the phone quickly. I stood and stared at it, unsure how I should have responded. The call felt intrusive and left an awful, foreboding taste in my mouth. With no experience to rely on, I put that feeling on a shelf. I had no clue what else to do with it, so I pushed it away and went to take care of my family.

As I tucked Samantha into bed and comforted her until she drifted off to sleep, I noticed up against the wall Emilie's donation box—still filled to the brim. My innocent girl, who only wanted to love and serve others, would never share that box and all of the valuable pieces of her life she put in it with others. The act that took her life was evil. My whole body became hollow, like a pit was opening inside of me, gaping wider and deeper. Then a stabbing pain burrowed deep into my chest and nestled somewhere in between my body and soul. This, I thought, was real grief. I kissed Samantha on the forehead. She was so beautiful and full of the kind of innocence that is supposed to help shield you from what is yet to come.

I went to bed but could not sleep. I got up alone and went to sit on the floor in Emilie's room where her absence was powerful and suffocating. With no distractions, the realization that she was gone hit me like a train. *I'm sorry I failed to protect you*, I thought, and felt my hollowed heart seize. I couldn't stand it; the pain was so great.

With nothing left inside, I went to my computer and found the memorial page my friends had started. I sat frozen and rapt seeing a photo of Emilie. Her gorgeous dark blue eyes—full of life—were looking right back at me. Other pictures showed her cheeky grin. Others captured funny moments she shared with friends and family. The images and the outpouring of connection and compassion, temporarily filling the empty shell of myself sitting at the computer. The agony I felt all day from an evil, evil act was now replaced with love and friendship. These pictures with accompanying messages, posted from those that knew her, were a sorely needed balm of solace to my painfully exposed heart.

"I remember her greeting me once saying, 'salutations.' She was four and it cracked me up. I'll miss you, Emilie."

"I still have the picture she drew for me at church once. She didn't know I was having a tough time, but her picture cheered me up. We love you, Parkers."

By the time sleep finally overcame me, a series of events was already well underway online and across the country—events that would reshape my family's future forever. Unlike Samantha, there was no chance that my naivete or innocence could protect me from what would happen next.

Chapter 2

The Press Conference

Any sleep I obtained was troubled and short-lived. Scenes from the previous day's events played over again whenever I closed my eyes, so I lay in bed for hours with them open. Feeling restless, I again went to our computer in the living room and opened Emilie's memorial page. The number of comments and messages had reached into the thousands overnight, mostly from strangers expressing their shock and condolences. All of them were sincere, but some felt like aloe on a fresh sunburn, providing just enough effect to soothe the pain for a second.

It was still dark when I went back and lay in bed next to Alissa. Throughout our marriage we had learned to lean on each other during hard times. She always knew how to ask the exact right questions and I loved her unique perspective. In a crisis she is a quick planner and my role of executing the logistics of a plan usually worked well. We had never encountered anything close to this before, so lying next to her that morning I wondered how this would test us, how it would change us. Once we both knew the other wasn't sleeping, we talked openly about how everything felt like a nightmare. That for a brief second after waking up, there was a doubt that any of it was real. But the nightmare sensation didn't go away.

When sunlight flickered through bare tree branches casting dancing shadows on the bedroom window, I felt utterly lost. Samantha was the first to join us when she crawled into our bed, followed shortly by Madeline and her pink blankie. We held each other in silence. I looked at my remaining two beautiful little girls, and felt so inadequate to address everything piling on top of us. I was scared how this tragedy would affect Madeline and Samantha. My heart ached with the knowledge that I had no idea how to help them navigate such a loss. The same with Alissa and our marriage. We'd heard statistics, long before the shooting, of how many marriages fail after the loss of a child. Emilie's death was like a meteor crashing into our own planet. How were any of us going to survive?

Overnight, Alissa's mother, sister, and brother-in-law flew in from Utah to stay with us. My mother also flew in early that morning but stayed at my little brother James's place a few towns over. He had recently moved to the area after leaving the Air Force to be close to us while working on his degree. Alissa's cousin from Brewster, New York, also came with her family that Saturday morning. It didn't take long for the household to stir awake after such a dreadful twenty-four hours. Our little family snuggle session that morning didn't last long, and would be the last such alone experience we would have for a long time.

As PROMISED, our church's leadership arrived at our home early Saturday morning, shaking off the bone-chilling cold outside and bringing needed warmth into our home that was filled with so much sadness. Dave Checketts was a regional leader for our church whom I had never met before he came to our house shortly after the shooting. An estimable man in every context, he was tall and athletic, with a tremendous résumé as a sports executive. With titles throughout his career as general manager of the Utah Jazz, president of Madison Square Garden, and owner of Real Salt Lake to name a few. I later learned that he first heard about the shooting while traveling to the airport to make a business meeting with his partner Jerry Jones of the Dallas Cowboys the next day. When he heard that a family under his stewardship was affected, he promptly canceled the meeting, turned the car around, and came straight to our home. I felt an immediate sense of relief when I saw him, because although he was a successful businessman, with six children of his own, he exuded fatherhood—exactly what I felt I needed that morning. Dave quickly got to work coordinating next steps with the logistics of transferring Emilie's remains to Utah and helped with planning funeral arrangements. Everything happened so quickly, we were still emotionally and logistically underwater, with little idea how to make our way out. His presence and decisiveness were a huge relief for us.

Alissa beelined to Deb, Dave's wife, with questions regarding our daughters. Deb, a licensed family counselor, came bearing gifts for Madeline and Samantha: two small stuffed dogs complete with miniature doghouses, stuffed treats, and toys. She presented them to the girls who were more than happy for a fun distraction amid the confusing gloom they must have been feeling. Deb explained that providing something the girls could take care of might provide them with a sense of control over something at a time when there was a loss of control everywhere else. Her loving warmth filled the room, along with a quiet confidence that said she was strong enough to handle anything. After the girls departed, Alissa's questions continued. "What behaviors should I be aware of with the girls? How do we make sure this doesn't negatively impact our marriage?"

Deb, on the other hand, had questions for Alissa. "Are you able to eat anything? Do you feel like you and Robbie communicate well?" Throughout the conversation, Deb helped clarify concerns and provided some sound advice. "Make sure you give lots of grace to each other. Take turns being the strong one as well as venting without taking personal offense."

Above all else, she made sure to make one thing very clear. Our girls would be looking to us for an example of how to react and respond to strong emotions. "They will emulate what you do and how you speak to each other," she said. "The best way to help your daughters and your marriage is to help yourselves." With that, Alissa and I understood clearly that any measure of our family's ability to survive was directly correlated to how we handled grief.

From then on, we made "healthy grief" our number one priority, knowing it was the best way for our family to endure and remain intact. We weren't sure what healthy grief meant for us exactly at that time. But I envisioned it looking like individual grief that was done together as a family. Of course, we would all grieve differently because Emilie meant something uniquely special to all of us. So, together, we would provide space, give grace, establish boundaries, go to therapy, and support each other's grieving process as a family. Alissa and I also vowed that we would always be honest with the girls. No matter what they asked or how hard something was to explain, we would tell them the age-appropriate truth. We didn't know much about what our new reality would entail. We knew grieving Emilie would be the hardest thing any of us had ever done, but we were committed to doing it together. What we could not have foreseen was the force coming toward us intent on preventing us from accomplishing just that.

Through social media, news of Emilie's death rapidly spread beyond close relatives and friends to others further outside our immediate circle. Before families were made aware their children had been killed, local and national media outlets descended on Sandy Hook with a ravenous appetite for *any* information regarding the shooting or victims. Every well-intentioned post someone made expressing condolences or remembering Emilie became breadcrumbs for fastidious reporters to follow directly to Alissa and me. By the following morning, the spread of information and the media's desire to consume it had already grown beyond anyone's control.

How could I have known that while I was speaking with my old high school friend Brad, media sleuths had begun uploading pictures from my Facebook page for their upcoming reports? I also didn't know that local news outlets were entering my older brother's house in Texas and my childhood home in Utah for interviews that aired the same night. But that wasn't enough. Every breadcrumb consumed only aroused the media's already excessive appetite for more.

As that Saturday morning rolled on, intense pressure from things being piled on us grew heavier. Our house was filled with mothers, in-laws, and siblings who were there helping us but also asking lots of questions. "Should I make some breakfast? Where are your pans? Do you want your cousin to arrange flowers for the funeral? You're low on milk . . . oh, and eggs. Robbie, what day should we fly back to Utah?"

Under the dark cloud of trauma and grief, my wife and I faced severe difficulty in making even the simplest decisions. Everyone thought of things we couldn't and stepped up to fill our family's needs. We were grateful they were there, but we were also exhausted and overwhelmed. Things were moving fast and I was struggling mightily to keep up.

All of a sudden, our landline began ringing. Alissa and I used our cell phones for everything; we only had a landline for emergencies. I didn't even know what my own home phone number was. The uneasy feeling I placed on the shelf the night before came back to me. Perhaps the police were calling for us? For the first time in history, I answered the awkward house phone, hoping it was a telemarketer.

"Hello! My name is . . . I'm a reporter with . . . I'm looking for Robbie Parker?"

I hung up immediately, feeling the same intrusiveness I had the night before. *Can't they just leave us alone?*

"Who was that?" Alissa asked.

"A reporter."

"Why? How did they even get that number?"

I just shook my head, remembering the *click click click click* from the day before. All I could feel now was appalled. Moments after the landline rang a second time, I reached over and pulled the cord out from the wall. But then there was a knock at the door and Alissa's cousin had to turn away a different reporter, who left flowers and a business card. When yet another reporter was asked to leave our doorstep, we became leery of any car that passed in front of our house. Then Alissa's cell phone rang. Her friend in New Mexico had been contacted by a reporter who saw her social media post the night before. She asked us how we would like her to respond. Similar calls started pouring in from friends and family in our home state of Utah, Oregon, and all across the country. Brad and Alan and their wives were contacted too.

"What do you want us to do?" they asked.

"I honestly don't know," I answered, completely exasperated.

"Even if you wrote up a statement," Brad said, "we could read it for you. We just feel uncomfortable speaking for you in any way without your permission."

"Hold on, I need to talk with Alissa. Let me call you back." Brad's call had given me an idea.

After our conversation with Deb earlier, Alissa had mostly remained still and quiet as the events unraveled around us. She is the most proactive thinker and doer I have ever been around, so her demeanor was not what I was accustomed to seeing and almost unsettling. Then I'd heard her own exasperation come through after someone asked her opinion about an arrangement. "I don't care," she'd snapped. "My daughter was just killed and I'm angry! I don't want to think about flights or schedules or eating or anything else. It doesn't matter."

Still, our phones kept ringing off the hook, mostly from reporters, making it impossible to get anything else done. Instead of being with Alissa or the girls, or even present and available to help plan how to get Emilie's body to Utah, I spent all afternoon on the phone dealing with the media situation. I was uncomfortable with how fast everything was escalating and worried that they wouldn't stop until they found someone that would say something. I knew that local outlets in Texas and Utah had already interviewed my brother and father, but truthfully, the idea of anyone talking about Emilie that weren't her parents did not sit right with me.

After Alissa's father died, three months before Sandy Hook, the local newspaper printed an article about his accident with information that wasn't accurate. Because of that, online comments under that article passed judgment on my father-in-law that was upsetting for his family. With that experience fresh in our minds, the last thing I wanted was for someone who did not know us very well to say something publicly about Emilie that was either erroneous or could be taken out of context.

With Alissa, her sister Jill, and brother-in-law Robby in the living room, I threw out an idea about providing a statement to the media under certain conditions. Jill and Robby felt like it could be a good idea while Alissa asked, somewhere between surprised and irritated, "Are you seriously considering doing that?"

I didn't want to, but I was also concerned about the pressure being put on our relatives and friends. I explained how uncomfortable I felt about someone speaking about Emilie without our permission and how I wanted to avoid a repeat of what happened with her father—though this time it would be on a much larger scale.

"Hopefully," I told them, "if we give the media a bone to chew on, they will stop pestering everyone and leave us alone."

After some more discussion we agreed to proceed with the statement under certain conditions. The plan we came up with was for me to meet with one reporter from a local station at our church that evening. I wanted it to be recorded, so that nothing could be misconstrued or taken out of context, then sent to Utah to be broadcast, since that is where most of our friends and family lived. That was it, one reporter, one camera, recorded and sent back to Utah.

We brainstormed things we felt were important to include in the statement, like portraying who Emilie was—and what the world was missing with her gone. Then Alissa said something that struck me: "That poor family. The shooter's family—can you imagine your child doing something like this? That must be so hard for them." At that time we knew nothing about the shooter or his family. Just that he was twenty years old and had once been a student at Sandy Hook.

It had been just over twenty-four hours without our little girl. Already such strong feelings of deep sorrow, grief, and pain were raging inside of me and Alissa. But we both knew that Emilie was the consummate example of unbounding love and compassion. She would want us to be her kind of example to the world, and to her two little sisters.

I pulled into the empty church parking lot an hour early. I found a classroom inside where I could be alone to gather my thoughts, and tried to pull myself together. I hadn't been alone much in the twenty-four hours since Emilie's death, but every time I was, my emotions overwhelmed me. Church leadership bustled about, setting out a podium in the parking lot and coming inside to check on me. Most of my family members arrived and did the same, except my brother, James, who was coming back from the airport with our father. Aside from Alissa, I needed my brother there the most.

Alissa planned to arrive right at five to watch and support but wanted to stay in the van with the girls at the back of the parking lot. When she arrived, she saw something I did not know from inside the church: the parking lot was full.

It was already dark when I exited the doors of the church into the chilly December air. In the hour since I had arrived, not only had the sun set, but dozens of cameras, reporters, and news crews had set themselves up in front of the podium. The moment I walked outside, I was disoriented by the bright lights and didn't know what to expect. I paused, expecting the one reporter who was called to come up and introduce themself to me, but no one came.

Nervously, I looked at my family and church leaders, who only returned blank looks back at me. Confused and feeling the tension building, I saw the podium and walked toward it, only then noticing all the cameras, microphones, and faceless people. It was all so surreal.

Trying to calm myself, I reflexively let out a weird, half laugh and smile toward some family there supporting me. The gesture didn't keep my heart from beating wildly when I finally reached the podium. The lights were blinding and *still* no one came to tell me what to do. So I asked the faceless void, "Should I start?"

Crickets. And so when no one answered, I simply took a deep breath, then let the words flow.

> So my name is Robbie Parker. My family is one of the families that lost a child at the Sandy Hook Elementary School shooting here in Connecticut.
>
> First of all, I'd really like to offer our deepest condolences to all the families who were directly affected by this shooting. It is a horrific tragedy, and we want everybody to know that our hearts and prayers go out to them. This includes the family of the shooter. I can't imagine how hard this experience

> must be for you and I want you to know that our family and our love and our support go out to you as well.

I paused, not wanting emotion to get the best of me, but the next words were hard to say without her here.

> My daughter Emilie would be one of the first ones to be standing and giving her love and support to all those victims. Because that is the type of person that she is. Not because of any parenting that my wife and I could have done but because those are the gifts given to her by her Heavenly Father. As the deep pain begins to settle into our hearts, we find comfort reflecting on the incredible person that Emilie was. And how many lives she was able to touch in her short time here on Earth.
>
> Emilie was bright, creative, and very loving. Emilie was always willing to try new things—other than food. She loved to use her talents to touch the lives of everyone she came into contact with. She was an exceptional artist and she always carried around her markers and pencils so that she never missed an opportunity to draw a picture or make a card for those around her. I can't count the number of times Emilie noticed someone feeling sad or frustrated and would rush to find a piece of paper to draw them a picture or to write them an encouraging note. Emilie's cardmaking was expressed beautifully this last October when she placed a very special card that she had made into the casket with her grandpa who also just recently died of a tragic accident.

This was something we hoped not only showcased how precious Emilie was, but also help everyone understand why we were not answering every single call that came in, even from people we loved so dearly. We were already crushed by grief before the shooting and even more now. Still, I continued:

> Emilie was a mentor to her two little sisters and delighted in teaching them how to read, dance, and find the simple joys in life. Emilie's laughter was infectious and all those who had the pleasure to meet her would agree that this world is a better place because she has been in it.

After finishing the statement, I tried to answer some questions before I began feeling awkward and realized that it was time to stop. Turning away from the podium, I found my little brother, James, for a hug.

"You did great, man."

"Thanks." I hoped Emilie thought so too.

I WENT STRAIGHT TO THE VAN to see Alissa and the girls. I was relieved it was over and hoped I had depicted Emilie's loving spirit well. Alissa told me she got text messages saying the speech had been aired live all over the country, but I only hugged her and the girls. I had done what I needed to do and was anxious to go home and be with my family.

It didn't take but a minute for us to discover that my idea to get the media off our backs bombed spectacularly. As I drove home, a reporter called my phone. "I'm a producer for *Good Morning America*. I just saw your press conference and wanted to ask if you would be willing to come on our show tomorrow morning?"

This time, I finally knew how to respond. "No thank you, I need to spend time with my family," I said shortly. "Have a good night."

More producers called and showed up to our door that evening. It turned out the bone I threw was gobbled up and swallowed whole while satiating nothing. Yet, I felt content now, knowing I did not owe the media anything. The path had been cleared for us to heal. It would be painful, but we would do it together. That evening Alissa and I snuggled with the girls on our couch downstairs as they watched a show, and we held them in our own fragility.

Unknown to us, back in Austin, Texas, Alex Jones and his team were in their war room, discussing how they could use this press conference to their advantage. They were looking for a target, and I had unwittingly stepped directly into their crosshairs.

Chapter 3

A New Dark World

Those few minutes, unknowingly caught on tape in front of the entire country, would follow me for the next ten years. Each time I saw it, I had the same string of thoughts, and when our lawyers played it on the first day of the trial, those thoughts were no different.

Seeing a screenshot of me "smiling" from an *Infowars* broadcast on the courtroom projector, I hung my head, eyes cast down. I was feeling something in between shame and anger. *How could you have been so careless?* I berated myself. I hated seeing that nervous and scared moment as I faced the media preserved on tape. For years, Alex Jones used those few seconds of me "laughing" and "smiling" to convince his audience that the Sandy Hook shooting was all fake. He told them I was a "crisis actor," getting into character. Meaning I was playing a role in cahoots with the government to purposefully stage this "fake" shooting as if it were real. In that moment the *they* he references so ambiguously materialized simply into me. To his listeners, I was not a grieving father—I became their mark.

I sat listening to our lawyer Chris Mattei give his opening arguments and wiped sweaty palms along my pants while my heart pounded inside my chest. Chris, a former federal prosecutor, was personable and affable off the record, but in the courtroom, he was sharp, methodical, and deliberate about everything he did. His shift in focus was palpable. I was no longer nervous and excited, eager to get things going, as I had been that morning when I first entered the courtroom. Now, while wringing my hands as the video clip played, I felt uneasy inside.

In the clip Jones used, there was nothing about my love for Emilie. No mention of her artistic talents or her bright personality. He stole and defiled the sincere, heartfelt tribute I shared about Emilie to satisfy his own greed. He erased my daughter and, for years, showed this doctored, five-second, deliberately slowed-down video of me on his website as a prop to sell his male enhancement and concentrated beet juice supplements to the tune of tens of millions of dollars a year . . . and to rile the tempers of his followers, who he turned loose on me.

THE MORNING AFTER I DELIVERED MY STATEMENT to the press, less than forty-eight hours since the shooting, I lay in bed, eyes open, still unable to sleep. Some emotions were starting to settle down and the truth of our new reality became inescapable as the house grew quiet. Alissa seemed to be navigating without a compass, like the piece of her guiding purpose was stolen. She remained present and in charge, but the pain was visible. Madeline and Samantha were a bright spot for us. They were old enough to be aware that something big was happening but innocent enough to still be themselves. Even if their childlike joy wasn't met with the usual authenticity Alissa and I could not muster at the time. The ache in my chest returned and, once again, I sought out solace from Emilie's memorial page so lovingly arranged by our friends. I hoped that the pictures and stories about Emilie would bring comfort and stop the repeated loop of events playing in my head. Instead, I was immediately assaulted by what I saw and read. Plastered all over her page were ugly comments I could not fathom.

"This shooting didn't happen, it's a complete hoax and you are a fraud."

This one was linked with an *Infowars* video depicting a crazed angry man I had never seen before in my life.

"Nice performance last night, you piece of shit crisis actor," another hissed, posting another link to an *Infowars* article.

What the heck is a crisis actor? I thought before reading another post.

"Who laughs and smiles after their daughter was supposedly murdered? Fuck you and fuck your daughter."

Shocked, enraged, and mostly disgusted, I switched the computer off, unable to comprehend what was happening . . . and why? I went back to bed but just lay there with this sickening feeling that I had done something horrible. I listened to Alissa's breathing. I knew she was awake, but I couldn't bring myself to tell her what I had just experienced. There was no expectation on how any of us *should* be feeling but it was also hard to read what the other was experiencing. Alissa's bright, energetic personality was subdued, her eyes muted. Which made it hard to determine if she was angry and needed space or wanted me to hold her in a way that said I was never letting go. I knew it was impossible to take away the anguish she was feeling no matter how badly I wanted to. The hardest thing for me was watching my wife and children suffer. It was more painful than my own misery, which was crushingly unbearable. Not only did I struggle to comprehend the loss of my daughter, but the guilt I felt about failing to protect Emilie was growing stronger. I doubled down on my resolve to protect my family. I decided to save them from seeing and feeling what I had just experienced. If only for a little while, I wanted to spare them what pain I could.

A few hours later, with the house still mostly quiet, I showed Alissa and her sister Jill the comments and posts from the memorial page. Alissa's shocked and disgusted reaction mirrored my own from earlier that morning. Jill went to the computer to get a better look at what I was talking about.

"These are just weird conspiracy theorists," she said. "They are the type of people that say the moon landing didn't happen or 9/11 was an inside job. They are just crazy people with nothing better to do." Thinking of them as just a few random crazy people somehow made me feel better for the time being. Perhaps, I'd overacted. Perhaps, my family was as safe as they could be.

That same morning, a list of all the victims was released to the public. After seeing the list, Alissa jumped up from the couch, grabbed something from the kitchen, then disappeared into the bedroom. I followed in pursuit finding her on the bed looking at a birthday party invitation Emilie had brought home the week before. Josephine "Joey" Gay, Emilie's autistic and non-verbal best friend, was supposed to celebrate her seventh birthday on Saturday, the day after the shooting. Alissa and Emilie had spent hours at the store carefully picking out the perfect gift, which remained wrapped on the counter in our laundry room. She picked up the phone and called Joey's mom. Despite all the people, love, and support surrounding our family, nobody knew exactly what Alissa was feeling, not even me.

When Alissa was in labor, Emilie's situation in utero became somewhat precarious. The doctor looked concerned and told Alissa, "Her heart rate is pretty low. She's not very comfortable in there and we need to get her out quickly." Alissa took his warning and instructions as a dare. With the next contraction, she gave every ounce of energy she had and delivered Emilie head to toe on one push! Even the doctor wasn't ready for that and literally had to make a basket catch, causing everyone to gasp. The labor team wrapped Emilie in a blanket and handed her to me and I was almost alarmed at how powerfully I loved her immediately. I had never experienced something so intense. When I handed Emilie to Alissa and watched them lock eyes together, I could feel their connection was even stronger than my own. I knew right away their bond was unique and eternal.

There was no way I could fathom what that loss felt like for her in those first few days. She needed another mom that could fathom that feeling. So, even though Alissa prayed that Joey wasn't hurt, when Alissa saw her name on the victim's list, she finally felt like there was somebody to talk to. Michelle Gay and Alissa had never met, but this phone call began a deep friendship that runs strong to this day. It was such a relief for Alissa to connect with someone who could understand what she was feeling right then.

"I don't know if you believe in heaven, but I do," Michelle told Alissa. "If you do, too, then I bet those two best friends are having the best party in heaven."

LATER THAT DAY, we received a call telling us that Emilie had left the state medical examiners and arrived at a funeral home outside Newtown. Alissa and I were thankful for a chance to be together and alone, if just for a little while.

The funeral director was kind, and we were surprised by how emotional he was while speaking with us. Despite everything he had experienced in his line of work, this event obviously touched him differently.

For my own processing, I felt it was important for me to understand the extent of Emilie's injuries. Since I couldn't protect her, I needed to know exactly how I failed her. This was information I did not want to obtain from the news reports shared by conspiracy theorists. In basic terms I asked the funeral director about Emilie's injuries. I wanted to see my daughter, and even speak with her again, if I could. He reassured me that it was possible if I desired. Alissa did not want to see Emilie in that state. She chose to keep all her memories of Emilie intact, including her bright blonde hair and deep blue eyes just as she had seen her last, full of life and love.

Everyone grieves differently and in that time we both spent precious and sacred moments with our daughter in the way each of us needed. Alissa seemed to be more in tune emotionally and spiritually. She was sensitive and reflective. I felt more reactive with my emotions without understanding really what they were trying to tell me. I was action-driven, with strong desires and less purpose. After our visit, we sat in the car together, wanting this experience to sink deep enough that we would remember it forever.

Driving away from the funeral home, Alissa called Michelle, Joey's mom, following through with a promise made earlier to update her about how things went at the funeral home. I watched as they poured their hearts out to each other. Alissa described what she felt at the funeral home. Not what she did, as I would have. It wasn't clear to me right then how much Alissa was able to genuinely express her feelings while I could only hold them in, without a proper outlet.

During their conversation, Alissa had to reject a call from an unknown number and complained to Michelle about how the media was relentlessly calling and coming to our door.

"What do you mean they are coming to your door?" Michelle asked. "Isn't your trooper keeping them away?"

"What are you talking about—a trooper?"

Apparently, the state police had assigned a trooper to be placed at the home of every victim. Michelle told us how their trooper stopped and questioned everyone that passed their house. Even her poor family members had to pass this scrutiny before being allowed down their driveway. It was via these troopers that communication between the town and the families was being conducted. "In fact," Michelle said to Alissa, "it was our trooper that told us President Obama is coming to meet with all the families."

"President Obama is coming?" Alissa responded, stunned.

"You didn't know? Yes, he wants to meet with all of us. We have to be at the high school in less than two hours."

Later, we learned that the state trooper assigned to us had also been assigned to another family. This simple oversight was an easy mistake, yet one that had left us vulnerable and exposed in a way that no other family was in those first two days after the shooting.

We called everyone at the house, telling them to get ready to meet the president as we tried to rush from the funeral home to our house in Sandy Hook—not an easy feat with an influx of people and cars descending into the small village. Upon our arrival, everyone in the house had to get ready in a flurry so we could get to the high school before the president.

Everything seemed so bizarre. In the last twenty-four hours I had unknowingly addressed the nation, was called a lying fraud, saw my daughter in a funeral home, and now the president of the United States was going to meet with us. *Why? What for?* I was so confused. All that other stuff, from media to conspiracists, was out there in the ether somewhere. This felt personal and intimate, and I couldn't wrap my head around the idea anyone outside of my close-knit circle would want to meet with us. It was like watching my old, familiar life violently break free from the orbit around my consciousness and float off into space, leaving whatever was left of me in a weightless vacuum with no purpose or meaning. I wanted to go back to Friday morning. I wanted the house to be quiet, the girls still asleep. As touched as I was that President Obama was moved to visit us, I just wanted my daughter back. Nothing around me felt like it was in my control anymore. Instead of being calm and collected, I was reacting to people telling me, "Do this . . . go here," while I lagged farther and farther behind wherever my emotions were dragging me.

As we hurried to get ready, Madeline asked Alissa for help putting on her "new" dress. I watched Alissa stop short, unsure if she could help Madeline with this simple request. The "new" dress was actually a very recent hand-me-down of Emilie's. We did a lot of that in our young family of three girls. Alissa told me later that she wanted to grab the dress and hold it tight to her face, not ready to lose any other part of her daughter yet. Not even her scent. With no time to spare and Madeline's sweet, determined face waiting, I watched my wife turn her tenderly around so Madeline wouldn't see her tears as she helped our four-year-old get into her fancy new dress. Seeing Madeline in that dress made me forget what I was doing and where I was. She looked so much like Emilie had, with matching blonde hair and sparkling blue eyes.

Our extended family group arrived at Newtown High School, with no idea what to expect from this experience. We soon found out President Obama would be meeting with all the families in small groups, not all together as I had anticipated. After Secret Service personnel found *Parker* on the list, we were ushered into the band room and told we would have to wait a while. I found a chair away from everyone, worn out, and just observed. Nothing made any sense anymore. I saw my parents, brother, and sister-in-law talking with Alissa's sister, brother-in-law, mother, and cousin's family. After the hustle and bustle, we were all left to wait for a long time. The room was very spacious, and the five children were playing, though thankfully not with any instruments. At one point I had to take one of the girls to the bathroom—a process that entailed notifying the Secret Service, who talked to someone who talked to someone who then approved the child's request. When we were escorted into the hallway, I saw President Obama about four doors down from ours speaking softly with some White House personnel before entering the room.

When President Obama finally entered our room, I didn't recognize the politician I was used to seeing on a television screen. His demeanor was unfeigned: he looked at us with sincere compassion and sorrow on his face. He approached me and placed both hands on my shoulders before hugging me.

"That was a courageous thing you did last night," he said, looking me in the eyes. Then he turned and hugged Alissa, saying, "I am so sorry about your beautiful daughter."

The moment he bent down to talk with Madeline, I knew why he was here. Not to fulfill some arbitrary obligation or score points for some stupid political scoreboard. He made Madeline smile, then he laughed with her. He came because he is a father before anything else. He was hurting with us, not just for us. The president made us feel that there was nowhere else he should be other than with us in a high school band classroom. It was personal for him. He spent time with everyone before he knelt back on the ground, all the kids surrounding him and smiling for a few pictures. He did not rush his time with us, and he repeated this process with all twenty-six families. I can't imagine the emotional toll that was for him. Afterward, he addressed a grief-stricken nation, but I wasn't there. By the time his speech was done, I was home helping the girls get ready for bed.

President Obama showed me in those few moments how to actually show up and be there for someone unconditionally and what it really means to be a father. He didn't care if I had voted for him a month earlier or not. He cared about us because he had children, daughters like mine. That night, as I tucked both my girls into bed, I liked to think that President Obama returned home to his girls and performed the same duties as I did. That at the end of every day, he and I actually had the same job and responsibilities. That we were fathers, first and above everything else.

As I lay awake again that night, though, I wondered, if the roles were reversed, would he be feeling as lost as I did? I was no longer the father I thought I was. I could already feel Emilie drifting away like on an ocean current, just out of reach no matter how strongly I fought the external forces to grab her hand. I had serious fears about the husband and father I would become. Would I become distracted, angry, withdrawn? I constantly worried about the version of me Alissa, Madeline, and Samantha were going to have because I didn't know what I was capable of handling or where my breaking point would be. From the first moment I became a father, I secretly felt inadequate to fulfill the role. Would I have the ability to show up now?

That night a relative innocently posted the picture of our children with President Obama on Emilie's memorial page. I didn't blame them, knowing most people would do the same—it was a big deal to visit with the president of the United States. On Monday morning, which was just three days after the shooting, hoaxers littered the page with a new conspiracy showing proof Emilie was still alive. These swindlers lifted an old family portrait from a blog Alissa used to write and set it side by side with the picture of little Madeline with President Obama. They made videos and displayed screenshots with yellow arrows pointing accusingly at Emilie and Madeline who were both wearing the same dress. "This," they claimed wildly, "is proof Emilie is alive because she is wearing the same dress from the portrait on President Obama's lap."

From then on, the memorial page was ferociously blitzed with screenshots of me smiling or Madeline wearing Emilie's hand-me-down dress. All associated with the most asinine comments, more links to *Infowars*, and interminable videos of Alex Jones.

As we prepared to return to Utah, where we would eventually bury Emilie next to her grandfather, the comments continued to roll in. Our plates were full figuring out the arrangements. When I had a moment in between packing and planning, I would check Emilie's memorial page. Every time I looked, it was increasingly diffused with more links, videos, and hate. I couldn't stand it. Even though I knew it was distracting me from focusing on what was really important in those moments, getting my family to Utah, I could not restrain myself. Those comments, to me, only confirmed I was inadequate to protect Emilie—in life or in death. This constant reminder drove me to a new level of despair.

My team of friends saw what was happening to the page they set up and recruited more administrators to help stifle the horrific posts defiling Emilie's memory, but to no avail. Good-hearted visitors to the page were also irate and engaged with the hoaxers to stop. This led to arguments and fighting as both sides dug in even deeper. My heart sank seeing this all play out. I pleaded with our supporters to stop engaging as any amount of contention did not embody who Emilie was. The memorial page had been turned from a place of emotional reprieve and solace into a war zone.

On Tuesday, four days after the shooting, when we finally left for Utah, we were trailed by a police escort from our home in Sandy Hook to JFK airport in New York City. Nobody mentioned anything about conspiracies being the reason, but I couldn't help but wonder. We did find out later that the FBI had been monitoring all the victims' families' homes and social media accounts for any dangerous or specific threats.

Pulling into the blocked-off curb at JFK, we were then greeted by airport security, taken through a special checkpoint, and placed in a private room before security walked us to our gate. In Utah, we exited the plane down the steps outside the jet bridge to a squad of more police vehicles waiting for us on the tarmac next to the plane, which drove us from Salt Lake City to our hometown of Ogden. I can't imagine the team it took to organize and plan all the logistical details for our trip, but I am so grateful to all of them that my family felt safe.

On the hourlong drive, I started noticing homemade signs hanging from overpasses expressing love and support to Emilie and the

Parkers. As we approached Ogden, we saw pink ribbons tied to lampposts and trees. The closer we got to Alissa's mom's house, more ribbons blossomed and flourished, filling up entire fences with banners and signs. The bright pink gave a pop of color against the snow-driven white canvas, something Emilie would have loved.

Back in our hometown, where we expected calm, everything only felt more intense. From the media, to conspiracies, to family issues, drama abounded all around. We appointed Alissa's brother, Brady, to be a contact person for any media-related issues. Which helped take some of the pressure off of me and Alissa. However, that didn't stop the media from contacting other family members who were unaware that any engagement or questions answered were "on the record" and used as such.

On one hand, it is hard to find people more loyal, nonjudgmental, loving, and willing to sacrifice for you than family. On the other hand, families are also full of a unique history that includes hurts, cover-ups, secrets, hierarchies, slights, assumptions, and grudges. My family is no different. Everyone was eager to help and kept wanting to take things off of my and Alissa's plate. Which only exacerbated my sense of loss of control when others made decisions on our behalf or took the girls for a drive without our permission. One evening, shortly after our arrival, the ever-pleasant Samantha got really upset and yelled at a cousin for trying to help her with something. This was so out of character for her that Alissa phoned Deb, the family therapist we met with the day after the shooting, and asked if we should be worried.

"No," Deb explained. "Everyone in your circle is hurting, and helping makes them feel better. Samantha, however, despite being only three years old, can detect if she is being used by someone else, even if it is well-intended. She is probably expressing, as best as she can, that she feels overstimulated by everyone helping her to ease her pain, which is totally normal."

At least the press and family issues were visible and you knew who you were dealing with. You could get help or talk to someone. The conspiracy issues, however, grew worse throughout the week as Alex Jones broadcasted two more Sandy Hook "special reports." During other broadcasts he spoke with on-air callers constantly about Sandy Hook, over B-roll video of me smiling, continually stoking the flames of the fire he ignited. We had no idea who or where these people were, putting us on constant alert.

Going out in public in any form was fraught with anxiety. In Newtown, our family was one of twenty-six; in Utah, we were one of one. Early that first morning after we arrived, Alissa and I grew nervous when two cars drove slowly by the house, twice. We were easily recognized by well-wishers who offered hugs and support. Although appreciated, it made me feel exposed and vulnerable. Out to lunch, later that afternoon, with our old high school friends, we all laughed when Alan recounted a funny story. I immediately caught myself, wiped the smile off my face, and scanned the room, feeling ashamed that someone might catch me smiling again. I feared someone might photograph or videotape me out of context and post it online to feed the miscreants. No matter where we were, it felt like we couldn't be ourselves. Healthy grieving people are allowed to laugh and smile when remembering their loved ones. Normal grieving people meet in small groups with trusted friends and family while most of the world leaves them alone. I worried that some random person from anywhere would judge me for not behaving exactly as they thought I should. Everything we did, said, or thought felt like walking through a minefield, littered with land mines based on lies.

Planning the viewing became increasingly difficult. Emotionally it was hard enough as I constantly felt like breaking down. Every day the rest of us moved forward was another day we were further away from Emilie. The reality of it was settling in as grief nestled into its new home inside my chest. Every little decision regarding the viewing we had to make felt like its own complete endeavor. A process further convoluted by many other opinions and insights that were not always asked for. Alissa worked on the slide show video that was to be played on loop for those waiting in line. We looked over Emilie's life captured through Alissa's amazing photography and bawled our eyes out the entire time.

On top of that, we had to make contingency plans after we heard rumors that a certain group, known for protesting outside of funerals, could make an appearance based on their objections to our Mormon religious beliefs. The idea of protesters spewing their hate and ignorance outside the viewing left Alissa and me shaken. If it were to happen, these wouldn't be nameless, faceless people elsewhere. They would be real people and in our faces and the faces of those that we loved most. Together with our family, Alissa and I were forced to question if we should even display pictures of Emilie or highlight her artwork. As most families would do to honor the life of their loved one. What if someone came through uninvited and took pictures of her things to post online as more conspiratorial proof? These all felt like threats to our family and the spirit of Emilie's viewing. Especially after we heard that people had crashed some funerals back in Newtown, and been caught trying to take pictures. Which forced us to make even more thorough security plans. I couldn't believe it. We were actually discussing the threat of protesters and security details for the viewing of an innocent, loving, six-year-old girl.

When Alissa and I arrived at the funeral home, a long line was already beginning to form outside the building. We tried to reset and be in the moment together. "This is about Emilie," we told ourselves. I didn't want to just get through the viewing. I wanted to be present so I could feel Emilie's spirit and the love her memory would bring together in that space.

The hall had become a wonderful display, personifying the life Emilie lived. Pictures, drawings, and crafts she made told her story. We let her light shine bright, without giving in to hoaxers. It was beautiful. After looking through one of her sketchbooks, I realized we were due to start in fifteen minutes. But when I looked around for Alissa, I couldn't find her anywhere. I checked bathrooms, the chapel, and offshoot rooms all over the funeral home.

Feeling frantic and wondering if I should raise the alarm with others, I finally heard Alissa in a coat closet behind the viewing area. She was crying, hyperventilating, teetering on the edge of a full-blown panic attack. I crawled inside next to her and shut the flexible accordion door.

"I can't do this, Robbie, I can't." She could hardly speak.

"I've got you," I whispered.

"I don't want anyone to do anything to her. I don't want this to be something used against us. I can't stand the thought of someone coming here, intent on tarnishing our daughter!"

I held her, letting her spill her anger and fear and deep sadness out. When others came by to tell us it was almost time, I closed the door and told them to wait as long as we needed. Then I went back and held her. I was worried and felt so unsure what I should do. There were no words to take anything she was feeling away. I knew we always leaned on each other when we needed support. So I pulled her close and held her and we cried together until breathing became easier and the evening felt doable.

"She deserves to be remembered and loved for who she was by those who knew her," I told my wife, caressing her cheek. "I will stay here, if you need to go. Everyone would understand."

"No, I can't do that," she said, taking a deep breath.

"Good, because I can't do this without you." We laughed for a second and then went out and faced the viewing together.

Hand in hand, we walked into the main room, to stand near Emilie's small closed casket. The line was huge. We were told it weaved all the way through the large funeral home, out the doors, and wrapped around the building.

In those hours as we hugged our family and friends, and traded stories of our favorite Emilie moments, I felt the most palpable sense of love I had ever felt in my life. During the viewing, my friend Jake, a gregarious, lovable teddy bear from my PA school, came through the viewing line. Then, about thirty minutes later, he did again.

"Just take a break," he murmured to us. "Stand here and hug me or don't, say something or don't. I just want to give you a break for a minute. Then I'll be back in a while for another."

Alissa choked back a sob and hugged him, thankful for the unexpected reprieve after holding herself so tight. I loved him even more after that for helping us get through a difficult evening. Though we had suffered the most horrific tragedy imaginable, I found that in that room amid all of the love Emilie inspired there was a flicker of hope. The agitators and their conspiracies were far from my mind; they were no match for this outpouring of ferocious love.

AND YET, AMONG ALL THE LOVING KINDNESS DISPLAYED, there was still so much evil hidden all around us, just waiting to make itself known. Within hours after Emilie's funeral, the following day, a video was posted to YouTube. It started with a picture lifted from a media website of our extended family leaving the church. The commentator zoomed in on me, smiling and waving, monologuing that when his dog died he cried for two weeks. Then protested, "And this sack of shit is smiling right after his daughter's funeral?"

When I came across this video sometime later, I remembered that moment vividly. My only niece from my side of the family, who I had yet to see since arriving in Utah, was moving through the crowd and yelled my name as I was about to enter the vehicle to go to the gravesite. I smiled and waved. Then blew her a kiss, got in the car, and started bawling. It was a beautiful memory and this man garnered tens of thousands of views tainting it.

We didn't feel safe. Our grief was robbed, and even openly sharing our memories put us at risk. I didn't realize the events from that first week after the shooting would fuel so many of my future choices and behaviors.

Chapter 4
Retreat

After spending over two weeks in Utah, we felt it was time to go back to Connecticut. With the funeral over, we had nothing to plan for or felt obligated to give anyone. The media attention abruptly disappeared, finally giving us space to breathe. Which also did not provide fresh ammunition for conspiracists to get their hands on. That didn't make them stop their socially metastatic pursuit, however. We had already begun approaching every decision we made through a lens of questioning if it could give someone something to use against us. Mostly, though, Alissa and I hunkered down as best as we could with our girls and close family. As the days passed and everyone else's lives slowly resorted back to some resemblance of pattern and normalcy, we realized it was time for us to do the same. On the red-eye flight home, with Madeline's head resting on my lap, I decided to zone out while watching some television—something I had not done since December 14. I hoped it would be a small taste of normalcy.

Scrolling through the channels, I came across something that startled me. The man I didn't know, but whose face I had seen time and again from conspiracy videos, was now staring wide-eyed at Piers Morgan on CNN. Piers wanted to talk about gun control, but Jones instead flew off the handle, screaming, "1776 will rise again!" The following day, that segment spread rapidly online, across social media, and was reported on nearly all news outlets. Ostensibly, we were back in Connecticut with the hope of beginning the slow road toward our new normal, but Jones was everywhere. All of a sudden, the anonymous comments had a face. And I was horrified.

Three weeks had passed since the shooting, and I thought that this whole conspiracy thing would fizzle out. I thought the trolls would move on to the next shiny object. But I couldn't have been more wrong. In early 2013, I didn't realize we were now in a social media age, where any one person had access to everyone else. Opinions once shared around the dinner table among close associates could now go viral in hours without a second thought.

The conspiracy chatter was no longer just online, and the rest of the world was catching up to what we had been experiencing constantly for weeks. Just as we were returning home, planning out how to support the girls as they went back to school, making plans for returning to work, the national media started contacting me again, asking for comments about a tenured professor named James Tracy, at Florida Atlantic University, who was giving lectures and writing blog posts about "The Sandy Hook Hoax." The conspiracy feral cat was now out of the bag and unfortunately, the more reporting done on the subject, the more vulnerable people were exposed to its twisted logic.

The fire Alex Jones started in Austin, Texas, had become a full-fledged wildfire that spread across the country. And for me, there would be no escaping it. As our lawyer Chris said to close his opening statement ten years later, "They had their memories, and Alex Jones turned those memories into a battleground."

Chris delivered his opening statement to a riveted jury inside a packed courtroom, except for the one empty seat at the defense table no one could ignore. The silence emanating from that vacant seat was deafening. As Jones's attorney Norm Pattis approached the jury, his white tennis shoes flashing beneath a dark suit. There was nothing he could do or say to hide the undeniable absence in the room. All through his opening remarks, the chair shouted louder and clearer demanding to know if Alex Jones would ever show up.

Jones did not appear until well after Mr. Pattis finished his statement. From the fifth-floor window, we watched as he and his entourage pulled up outside the Waterbury Courthouse in a number of black SUVs. He exited with bodyguards flanking him on either side while he approached a bank of microphones and cameras to give a press conference where he railed against the judge and this "kangaroo court," moaning and wailing in full victim mode. His face progressed in shades from light pink to beet red. He claimed mistreatment, denial of his due process, and of all things, that he was being silenced.

The media with their cameras and microphones digitally gobbled up each regurgitated morsel from his mouth, like featherless baby birds that remained insatiable until the next feeding came. It was a despicable scene, displaying their willingness to provide Jones with unfettered publicity to spread his message and lies to even more people, whenever he wanted to.

But inside the courthouse, we could sense that the tide was changing—and Jones knew it. For all of his pomp and bravado, he was scared. For four years Jones balked at accountability and tried everything he could to avoid this trial. He hired, fired, rehired, and fired lawyers time and again, he stalled, he ran away from depositions, he appealed rulings and claimed bankruptcy—twice. Every tactic he deployed to avoid this trial failed. Now he was forced to accept that he couldn't hide anymore. But like a true bully, he came, puffed his chest, screamed, threw insults, and then retreated.

When the diatribe was over, his bodyguards escorted him back to the SUVs and he left, without ever entering the courthouse. He was following the same pattern that put him in this position to begin with, doing the only thing he knew how to do—lie. He lied from outside the courtroom into cameras as easily as he did in his studio—soulless cameras that couldn't hold him accountable. "What a coward," someone muttered as we watched him escape to higher ground, marooning his defense attorney to sink or swim.

Inwardly I cringed, knowing his spineless departure felt eerily reminiscent of my own actions. For too long, I lied to others that Jones's antics had no effect on me. I couldn't let anyone, including myself, believe these people had any power over me. I couldn't give them that satisfaction. This perceived stoicism, in reality, was only a way to escape the truth of what was happening to me. But I'd arrived in the courtroom ready to finally defend my truth.

At the beginning of the trial, I assumed Jones's lawyer was there to do the same. I sincerely believed that Norm Pattis was a lover of the law, seemingly fueled by a strong belief that everyone deserves to be represented by legal counsel—that even the most despicable person must be entitled to a defense. I understood and completely respected all of those principles. But it wasn't long before he proved me wrong.

Instead of establishing a defense, Mr. Pattis instead chose to continue his client's defamatory narrative. Waving his hands, with the jury's undivided attention, he emphatically pointed out that, "Adam Lanza killed their family members—not Alex Jones," before pausing for dramatic effect. "They want to be compensated for their grief. Money is their weapon of choice. They are asking you to do with money . . . what most of us do at home when we hear something we don't like—we turn off the TV set."

A cold chill ripped through me at his words. *What the hell—is he serious?* I knew I wasn't going to agree with what Norm Pattis would say or his strategic approach. But for him to assert that we were trying to make Alex Jones pay for Adam Lanza's murders? That was too far beyond the pale. I was furious, my jaw clenched tight. Alissa, also angered but sensing my level of distress, patted my hand reassuringly.

He continued, "They have exaggerated their claims that Alex Jones caused them harm and transformed their grief and rage over the death of a loved one into a powerful and effective motive . . . for money." Then he tried to impersonate Alex Jones, highlighting one of Jones's most notorious comments, "*chemicals in the water turn the freakin' frogs gay.*"

"At what point," Pattis asked, "do we consider Jones a crank on the village green? A person that we can walk away from—if we choose to?"

I was baffled and deeply offended. The gall Pattis possessed to insinuate to the jury that we somehow *chose* to be harmed because we didn't "change the channel" or walk away from Alex Jones's broadcasts, or that we somehow exaggerated the negative impacts Jones's actions had on our lives were astounding to me. Mr. Pattis's whole line of reasoning was darkly manipulative.

"Walk away—if we choose to? Screw that!" I whispered to Alissa when Mr. Pattis was finished with his statement. *Change the channel, ignore, walk away,* I thought to myself. *What does he think I've been doing this whole time?*

From the morning after the shooting, all Alissa and I wanted was to focus on our family's grief and healing. We began meeting with Deb Checketts regularly as a couple and individually. Alissa was doing better at working through the anguish and despair brought on by Emilie's death. In late January 2013, Alissa started writing a new blog where she processed her grief journey. Initially this was only for herself, but close family members were eventually allowed to receive posts. After some encouragement she allowed the blog to become public, but did not allow comments of any kind. Her writings were raw and beautiful expressions of everything from her deep sadness to small victories. Every post was accompanied with her exquisite photographs visually highlighting what she saw, felt, and remembered. What she shared touched and helped many people as Alissa opened a window into the grieving process that was relatable and not overwhelming.

On the other hand, I felt incompetent to process the gravity of my emotions. While Alissa opened herself up and shared, I turned inward and focused on something that appeared more tangible, protecting my family. My online surveillance expanded beyond Emilie's memorial page, to actively searching for content that might pose a risk or threat. This fear circled through my mind constantly, that if I didn't know what was out there, then I wasn't prepared for what could be coming. This approach was futile, as conspiracy content about me and other Sandy Hook parents multiplied every day. A simple Google search found thousands and thousands of results, with *Infowars* and Jones usually claiming the top spots. Unable to keep up only perpetuated the rumination that I was failing to keep us safe. It was a vicious negative feedback loop, but I couldn't stop. Because I didn't know who Adam Lanza was before he killed his mother and twenty-six other souls on December 14, 2012. I never fathomed that someone I didn't even know existed, from our own community, was capable of inflicting so much pain and suffering. Logically, I understood there was nothing I could have done to stop him, but still, those feelings of guilt and remorse kept me up at night, and were compounded by the fact that I was now perfectly aware of what one stranger was capable of doing to another. I saw it. I felt it.

Eerily, I also didn't know who Alex Jones was before the shooting. Yet, within one day of the shooting, he and his millions of followers knew who *I* was, and he gave them a reason to hate me.

After we returned to Connecticut from Utah, the conspiracy messages had graduated past online anonymous posts to sending physical letters to my home. And not just our home: a majority of Sandy Hook families received threatening material in some form or another. The FBI eventually was forced to assign a small team whose sole purpose became investigating Sandy Hook conspiracists and tracking down any reasonable threats. We were all given direct contact information for an agent and were informed on what kind of communication rose to the level of being reported.

Once back in Connecticut, we tried our best to put wind into our grief-processing sails. Madeline returned to preschool, Alissa was blogging, and through therapy I was working on trying to be more present and had a blast at a dino-dig day activity with Madeline. Each of these occurrences were small wins in what felt like an insurmountable struggle. It wasn't much but it felt like those sails had caught a breeze. However, shortly after our FBI meeting, Alissa and I read an actual letter where one man articulated his fantasy about what my head would feel like after blows from his baseball bat. The letter knocked any wind out of our sails. We sat eyes wide on the couch staring at each other, chilled to the bone. We had no words but we both knew we felt the exact same way. Our home no longer felt like ours. Actually, holding that letter broke the fourth wall between us and them. This wasn't through a screen from someone out in the ether anymore. A real person found out where my family slept every night. It wasn't just scary, it was tangible. It was dangerous.

After the shooting, now knowing full well what one person could be capable of doing made every one of these dealings vividly real for me. Then there was the fact that Adam Lanza didn't know me and he didn't hate Emilie specifically. These people did, and they didn't mind demonstrating that they knew how to find us.

These experiences, however, went beyond just my immediate family. They spread to our friends and extended family as well. Brooke, our friend who had started the memorial page on Facebook, answered her phone one January afternoon to an unpleasant surprise. Without identifying himself, a man asked if he was speaking to Brooke. Then he asked if she was friends with Robbie Parker. His voice then turned demanding, asking her how they were able to set up a fund and ask for money before the shooting even happened. Before Brooke could react, his voice turned into venom spitting in her ear: "You people make me *sick*!" Then he launched into a nonsensical rant about other "fake" shootings and people who are hell-bent on destroying the freedoms of citizens. Later, when recalling this moment to me, Brooke described, "My mind and body were immediately flooded—and made me want to throw up."

Brooke's experience filled me with guilt for having exposed my friends to this kind of harassment. *Come after me all you want,* I thought. *Just leave my friends and family alone.*

I watched other Sandy Hook family members get eviscerated nearly every time they did or said something publicly. One father was heckled relentlessly while providing testimony on the impacts of gun violence to the Connecticut general assembly. YouTube, with its algorithms, was very adept—and invasive—in suggesting a mile-long list of conspiracy videos, highlighting other Sandy Hook families' "odd behavior," complete with special effects, sinister music, and common themes like, "*Protecting Our Freedoms*" and "*Good Versus Evil.*"

For more than three and a half weeks after Emilie's murder, our family rallied around each other. By the fourth week, I felt like it was time to return to work. Not only could our young family ill-afford me off work for long, I desperately needed to throw myself into something that wasn't about me or us. What better way to do that than to work with innocent, premature babies needing a special level of care? I craved any feeling of normalcy and to see if I could find some semblance of my previous life.

My desire, though strong, was initially combined with trepidation. *How will I feel,* I wondered, *when I attend a delivery and watch a happy family embrace their new baby girl? How will I react? Will it be with joy . . . or indignation? Will I be able to control my emotions if I feel overwhelmed?* These thoughts scared me.

I didn't want to place myself in a position, especially in an intensive care situation, feeling unsure how I would respond. Rationally, I understood these unsettled feelings were a natural expression of processing grief. *How does my new abnormal situation coincide with another's normal experience?*

I decided to call Deb Checketts, who by now was used to fielding texts and calls from Alissa and me. I told her how nervous I was feeling about how I might respond to all the different scenarios and pressures that come with my job.

This was unlike anything I'd ever experienced in my career. Being a NICU physician's assistant demanded outward focus, compassion, and presence—skills I used to possess but wasn't sure I still had.

She answered my questions assiduously and counseled me not to resist any emotion that comes up, "or it will persist." If I started to feel overwhelmed at a time I needed to focus, then she advised me to reground all my senses. "Hold your stethoscope, take a deep breath, press your feet into the ground, listen to the baby's cry, smell . . . whatever it is you smell there. I'm sure it's not always pleasant." This advice helped alleviate my nerves that evening and seemed simple enough to follow.

The next morning, I arrived at work with butterflies in my stomach, not knowing what to expect. In direct contrast to the ugliness on social media, when I entered the NICU I was greeted by friendly faces and caring people. It was awkward at first, the familiarity of it all. The people, place, and setting were all the same—but everyone knew *I* was different. Soon, I noticed we had all changed.

As great as it was to be around everyone again, I could feel a shift in how people were responding to me. After initial greetings, I left to change into my scrubs, where I had to walk through the labor and delivery unit. When I opened the double doors a group of six nurses were grouped together talking. One nurse let out an audible gasp and walked away. Three were surprised and rushed over to welcome me back. While the remaining two seemed to remember something they forgot to do and made themselves busy. These different reactions made me realize that just me being there impacted people in different ways. My job had always been a comfort zone for me, a place where I felt comfortable to be myself. Now, based off everyone's reactions, I didn't feel that way anymore. This was the first time I recognized how this tragedy had impacted other people outside of family and friends. It felt like that realization of deep loss in our community was a struggle everyone was trying to grasp and understand. It affected and changed all of us profoundly. Then me and my loss being back meant we all had to face the uncomfortable together, which caught us all by surprise.

Early on in that shift, the first call came through for me to attend a high-risk delivery, and I heard Deb's voice in my head, *deep breath . . . feel . . . listen . . . smell . . . okay.* I felt ready to handle whatever came my way. As I approached the delivery room door, another thought, unbidden, screamed over Deb's counsel. *What if they are conspiracy nuts? Freak, what are you going to do if they recognize you?*

I stopped outside the door while my team rushed into the room. I hadn't anticipated this freezing paralysis. More panic and fear rose with the mere thought of a potential confrontation. Alone in the hall, I whispered to myself, "It's okay," *deep breath*, "the fear is okay, but you have to go in there," *deep breath*. "The baby might need you and that's *all* that matters now." Another deep breath and I clutched my stethoscope. "You've got this—you ready?" With a final breath, I felt the corners of my mouth tug up a little, because if I can smile, nothing is too big to handle.

I heard the mom yell inside the room, with everyone cheering her on, "*Push!*" Then I opened the door and joined my team. Within moments the baby was delivered and placed on the bed warmer in front of me. I saw her and she was beautiful! I rubbed her back till I heard her cry. Using my stethoscope to listen to her lungs, I let her grab my fingers. The father had tears streaming down his face but in joy, and the mother was relieved at the sound of her baby girl's throaty scream. So was I.

It became hard for us to do "normal" things. Running necessary errands, dropping off the girls at preschool, going to the post office, simple activities that would have given our lives a small semblance of normality, were all opportunities for uncomfortable, though well-meaning run-ins. Alissa and I were consistently stopped by lovely, caring people who wanted to share their condolences, tears, and support for our family. We focused on these beautiful strangers and their compassion and vulnerability, which I found admirable. These interactions could be emotionally uplifting on many days. They could also be emotionally taxing on harder ones. It was another reminder that our old lives were things of the past.

After one such encounter at IKEA, Madeline asked me, "Why do people come up and hug you all the time?"

We shared that there are wonderfully caring people everywhere. We didn't tell her about the ugliness on social media or in letters sent to our doorstep. Nor did we tell her about the gut-churning fear we felt each time a stranger locked eyes with us. Was it someone who remembered Emilie's bubbly giggle and wanted to share one of their memories of her with us? Or would it be someone who didn't believe Emilie existed at all? The uncertainty turned even the most mundane interactions into high-stakes interrogations. Soon, I dreaded leaving the house. Because of the press conference, I was more easily recognizable than Alissa when in public. Which caused the girls and even Alissa to feel uncomfortable running errands or going places with me if they didn't have to. One time I heard Alissa ask Madeline if she wanted to go to the store with her. "Is Dad going?"

"No, Dad is staying here."

"Okay, then I'll go with you."

On one particularly hard day, Alissa and I decided to drive to a Target two towns over, hoping the distance from Newtown would provide some level of anonymity. We parked and made it halfway from our car to the store when we passed a woman staring at us. Avoiding eye contact, I quickly steered Alissa and me around her, trying to create a buffer space between us before she asked, "Aren't you Robbie and Alissa, Emilie's parents?" as she quickly bridged the gap I had just created.

"Hi, yes we are," I answered politely, slowing my pace while trying not to stop completely.

"I can't believe it! The chances of running into you today!" Suddenly, she started crying, so Alissa and I stopped, right there in the parking lot. "I'm so sorry, she was so beautiful . . . I'm sorry I'm crying. My husband is a paramedic," she explained quickly, "and he is so distraught by what he experienced that day."

"Oh my gosh," I replied sympathetically, worried about what her husband may have seen and how it may have affected him.

She pressed on, "I don't know how you guys can cope with what happened that day. My husband is so mad because he wasn't allowed into the school when he arrived. It bothers him because he *could* have done something to help, but they wouldn't let him in."

With this latest pronouncement, the feeling between us began to deviate from shared compassion. *Not this, not today . . . please,* I thought.

"How can you stand that they didn't allow paramedics into the school after the shooting?" she asked tearfully, her words laced with a torrent of anger. "I'm sorry they didn't let my husband in; he might have been able to help Emilie."

I could hear my pulse pounding in my ears listening to what she was saying. I didn't know if this woman was a conspiracy theorist assuming her husband being barred from the school was an act of ill intention from the government or if she was a slightly misinformed, but well-intentioned, neighbor. Either way, I had to make it stop. "I'm sorry your husband is having a hard time—please thank him for his service; we know he did all he could. I hope you have a nice day," I added as politely as possible, before taking Alissa's hand and continuing our trek toward the store.

We'd heard that on the day of the shooting, scores of first responders arrived on scene—too many to be utilized. That, mixed with the active crime scene, meant many responders who arrived later than others were not permitted access to the school. This very logical response was picked up by conspiracy theorists claiming "they" were hiding something. One of many conspiracy videos on this topic claimed the "they" loud and clear:

> Why did they not allow paramedics to enter the school? Because they couldn't allow anyone not in on the ruse to see that nobody was killed. Could you imagine being a first responder to a mass shooting and not see any blood or dead children? Like *they* claimed? If you're not a crisis actor or an Obama-loving government official, then you weren't allowed to see the truth.

Although the paramedic's wife was sincere and sympathetic to our loss, the interaction was disturbing. It demonstrated how a simple, logical truth could be warped into something much more sinister and yet still be absorbed by those you'd least expect. It showed us that more people believed in this than we'd realized, and that try as I might I could not just go and "change the channel" in the middle of the Target parking lot like Norm Pattis would later ridiculously imply.

As the weeks progressed and the online hatred became worse, it was impossible to know who was imbibing this misinformation—or on which part of the conspiracy spectrum they fell. But no matter what someone's intentions were—an accidentally misinformed neighbor or a malicious instigator—my sense of trust and safety was eroded. I felt I could not extend the benefit of the doubt in even the most innocuous interactions. At the grocery store, at work, I found myself suspicious of everyone. I felt I couldn't afford not to be. I had to protect my family.

The woman in the Target parking lot was sincere but confused between real and altered facts. The person that sent me a Facebook request from a profile they created as the shooter, Adam Lanza, complete with his picture and demographics? That was cruel and malicious. What we wished we didn't have to know was that others were outright dangerous.

When the topic of conspiracies and hoaxers came up with other Sandy Hook families, it was done mainly in a dark humor kind of way. One evening after a state police report briefing on their investigation, Nicole Hockley and I joked around about how I was part of the illuminati and willingly sacrificed Emilie while also being told that Emilie never existed; while she told me stories of how she was accused of not only sacrificing her son Dylan, but also sold her body to the elites as admission to participate in this great conspiracy. Together, Nicole and I could laugh about the absurdity of it all. But we also didn't share with each other how we actually felt or open up about how this could be impacting us. She didn't talk to me about reports she may have made to the FBI, nor did I tell her how scared I was at times for all of us. For some reason, those issues felt deeply personal, and we kept them close.

For months it felt like no matter what we did or where we went we were hit with another bombshell or inadvertently triggered another unseen land mine. All I wanted was one day, one afternoon even, where I could just feel normal again. I craved at least some semblance of my old self that could orient me to who I used to be because I wasn't sure anymore. It felt like I was going to burst if I couldn't get even a brief reprieve from this foreign dimension we had all been thrown into. In late February, just over two months since Emilie's light was snuffed out, I received a phone call from the most unlikely of places.

There was no way I would answer an unknown number, but I'll never forget listening to the voicemail. "Hello, my name is Chuck Morgan from the Texas Rangers . . ." as only a stadium announcer can sound. Chuck Morgan has been the public address announcer for the Texas Rangers for more than thirty years. I grew up in Arlington, Texas: I recognized his voice from games I went to as a child and now he was on my phone, but why?

After Emilie died, the media snatched my profile picture from Facebook and used it as part of their portfolio Rolodex whenever talking about Sandy Hook victims. The picture showed a beaming Emilie, holding a baseball high in the air with me standing behind her wearing a Texas Rangers hat. That picture was taken at Fenway Park, earlier that spring, after we watched Alissa's dad run in the Boston Marathon.

We arrived at the game early that day for batting practice. I had spent the day teaching Emilie all about batting practice and how it was the best chance for us to get a baseball. After we arrived, Emilie asked, "How many balls do we need to get so everyone with us can have one?" She was five years old at the time, thinking of everyone else. I was thirty and didn't care about anyone else because I was still waiting to get my first baseball at a game.

As the players rotated through batting practice, Emilie and I waited in the right field stands hoping for a ball that felt like it was never coming. Then David Murphy, a left-handed-hitting outfielder for the Rangers, hit a ball deep to right field and over the crowd of people behind the Red Sox bullpen. The ball smacked against an empty chair to the right of Emilie and me. I saw a young boy around ten years old running toward it, which released my ten-year-old inner self (but with the stride of a thirty-year-old), and I snatched the ball from right in front of him. The crowd adamantly booed me, an adult with a Rangers hat, stealing from a little boy wearing a Red Sox cap. That is until they saw Emilie running toward me jumping up and down screaming, "*We got one, we got one!*" She took the ball from my hands and lifted it high in the air, eliciting cheers and changing hearts in the crowd around us. As always, Alissa captured the perfect picture.

I quickly called Chuck Morgan back and sputtered something about me being who I am. Chuck thanked me for calling back and got straight to the point. "We had a meeting this afternoon discussing Opening Day, and I wanted to invite you and your family to be our special guests and throw the first pitch—for Emilie." He continued, "You don't have to answer me right now—we want to be mindful of everything you are going through. Take some time, talk it over with your wife, and you can call me back."

Even though I didn't need to think it over, I love that he gave us the space to do what we felt was best for us. Already in those first few months, so many people, groups, media, and politicians wanted us to use our story to further their cause or purpose. The Texas Rangers had no ulterior motive. All they knew was that they had lost one of their fans and they wanted to let her family know they thought she was special.

In April 2013, my family arrived in Arlington, Texas. Being back where I grew up filled me with more emotion than I had anticipated. I took my girls past my old house, old school, old church . . . places where a six-year-old version of me rode his bike around carefree with no concerns about the life ahead of him. It hurt thinking of all the things I had experienced in my life from then till now—things that Emilie would never experience.

The support from the community was amazing. The Sandy Hook tragedy is such an intimately personal thing for me that I really fail to grasp its effect across the country. Rangers fan clubs hosted fundraisers for a non-profit we were starting in Emilie's honor. Newspapers wrote wonderful tributes. This was one of the few times where I saw how the tragedy touched others' lives and they seemed eager to rally around and support us. Not with thoughts and prayers from afar, but with real face-to-face words, real hugs, real BBQ, all in a genuine Texan way. Along with all of that, family and my best friends from Utah came to support us in this once-in-a-lifetime opportunity.

As all this love and support came pouring in, I suddenly felt that there was so much more to this pitch than some symbolic ceremony. For me it was to honor Emilie—she was why we were there. It was also a way to show everyone our sincere gratitude for the love and support that was so freely given. I began to feel pressure that this gesture of throwing a baseball could somehow symbolize my appreciation for everything everyone had done for us, and I didn't want to let them down by bouncing it in the dirt.

When opening day came, it was anything but a normal experience. I met childhood heroes and baseball legends like Nolan Ryan and Pudge Rodriguez. President George W. Bush gave me advice to "aim high and don't bounce it," as his wife, Laura, let Samantha crawl all over her lap and grab her face while she talked with Alissa on a couch. We walked out onto the same field I pretended to win World Series games on as a little kid in an empty field behind my house.

David Murphy, who hit that batting practice home run, met us on the field, with his signed jersey from the season opener. He had become Emilie's favorite player, and to this day I appreciate his friendship.

Finally, it was time to throw the pitch. All I remember is letting the ball go and realizing it was heading to Pudge's glove and wasn't going in the dirt. All the tension and pressure I was feeling was gone and before I knew it Pudge pulled me into the most muscular embrace I've ever felt. It was an amazing moment.

With all that craziness behind me, I could finally do what the Rangers wanted for us all along. By the second inning, I was sitting in the stands next to my little brother, James, surrounded by friends and family, enjoying a ball game. This was a chance to just let go. Let go of the pressure, let go of the expectations, let go of everything that had been invading my life and not feel guilty about it. I almost forgot that I didn't need to feel guilty for laughing, cheering, or eating a hot dog and could allow myself to be content in the present moment.

For the next seven innings, I briefly felt like my old self again. This reprieve from all the heaviness in our lives at the time was more than welcome. It was nice to have something to look forward to. A healthy distraction to remind you that good times are still to be had. That feeling of lightness, love, and joy is not only possible but sparks a desire to seek more of it. My problems and the hard road ahead of me could not be thrown aside like that pitch. The Rangers, fans, community, friends, family, and even God cannot take any of that away from me, nor should they. That would rob me of my growth and process. But they can help carry it, even if only for an afternoon.

MONTHS AFTER THE SHOOTING, two FBI agents sat at our kitchen table and meticulously read the piece of paper I handed them. The letter sat on the far end of the conspiracy spectrum. Its contents confirmed that this was the same person who had called our friend Brooke and made her want to vomit. Now, four months later, the letter held other verifiable facts and information that the FBI could actually work with. The trail they followed revealed someone with a long history of harassing victims and families from mass shootings, including the Aurora, Colorado, theater; Virginia Tech university; and the Sikh temple in Oak Creek, Wisconsin. Those were not the only ones.

Absolutely resolute in his beliefs that the massacres at Sandy Hook and these other events never happened, he first harassed and scared our friends, and was now coming after us.

One of the agents looked up at me. "How far do you want us to take this?"

"As far as it leads you," we answered. This entire experience felt like an alternate reality. We lived in this house, but it wasn't a home anymore. Everything felt gray and hopeless. We just wanted to be left alone, but we couldn't, and now the FBI was involved. Alissa later told me it was after this meeting she first felt that we needed to move away.

The impacts of these events on myself and my family were sometimes unseen, but always felt. The shame I carried that everything conspiracy related impacting the entire Sandy Hook community was my fault, along with the constant reminder of my perceived failures, was crushing. The more shame I carried, the more it felt impossible to talk about it with anyone, including Alissa. When asked how I felt, I lied. "I'm fine." "I've got this." "Don't worry, I'll take care of it." Alissa knew this wasn't true, but every time she brought up what she saw in me or how she felt, her loving concerns were met with rejection fueled by shame and fear. Unsure how to approach me in a manner that could be accepted, Alissa gave me space to work through these issues on my own. However, the more I lied about this to myself, the more frustration, shame, and fear built up inside of me.

Throughout this time, we constantly strove to meet each other with understanding, love, and respect, as we agreed upon from the beginning. And we succeeded many more times than we did not. Emotions, when expressed, were met without judgment or criticism. When anger was expressed, it was never directed at anyone but rather talked about or vented toward the culprit of the strife.

This must have been such a confusing time for Madeline and Samantha, now five and four years old. They were doing their best to understand complex and heavy emotions they felt around the house, and in themselves, while reading confusing body language as best they could. Many days they were as carefree and joyful as ever. But Alissa and I were also trying to read them and follow their lead on what support they might need while questioning every day if we were doing enough or messing up all the time.

Fortunately, within two months, the FBI caught and arrested the author of that letter, three thousand miles away, in Portland, Oregon.

For morale reasons, the arrest in Portland felt like a big win for us. In reality, it was only the equivalent of hitting a single to break up a no-hitter in a 10–0 blowout. Between December 2012 and that man's arrest in April 2013, I tried everything I could to stem the onslaught of harassment and threats . . . to no avail.

Toward the end of January 2013, Emilie's memorial page became so inundated with vile filth and lies that we were forced to shut it down for a period of time.

"How is Emilie tonight? We know the bitch is alive or never existed."

"You dirty no good son of a bitch we know Emilie never existed and you just collect money."

"You will have to answer to God for your bullshit! Your kids are ugly! You punk bitch!"

It was so demoralizing. How could I compete with this propaganda machine and the fervor it allotted? *How could I ignore this man and also fulfill my obligations to protect my family?*

We did everything we could to get Facebook, Twitter, and YouTube on our side, hoping they could implement policies to slow, if not stop, the spread of these conspiracies. Alissa's cousin used to work for a high-powered public relations agency out of New York. His former boss (and vice president of the company at the time), Marian Salzman, came to bat with us in our battle against the malignant spread of lies and conspiracies. With her help, our pleas were elevated to the highest echelons at Facebook. We weren't aware but at the same time other families through their own contacts were also fighting against social media giants. Our individual crusades were all met the same way, with typical corporate responses that began with, "After careful review . . ." or deafening silence.

No matter how high I climbed or how far I yelled, nothing seemed powerful enough to overcome the stacks of money Alex Jones's content brought to these platforms. Or, as I felt, my voice, my family, and our safety was worth nothing compared to the financial gain that came from disseminating outrageous conspiracy theories.

With seemingly no barriers in place, the tidal wave of misinformation continued to flow inland, totally unimpeded. It was freakish how one conspiracy would birth others that would then mutate until it became unrecognizable from the original parent conspiracy. In their world, Emilie was still alive, never existed, or I willingly sacrificed her in a zealous pursuit to rid the country from guns. They all bragged about doing individual research and reaching unique conclusions while all sounding the same. Yet, despite all this work and sleuthing, they never did reach the most logical conclusions or come across any of the actual evidence that was readily available to them.

Finding no recourse from the social media companies left me feeling completely abandoned. It was demoralizing to feel that I was left to battle these forces alone. Without any tools at my disposal, the only approach I saw was that information was power, so I remained engaged about what misinformation was being spread. However, this fight left me feeling like I was diverting precious water from a natural river into a man-made canal, leaving my natural ecosystem thirsting for needed resources while watering an artificial landscape. And it became clear to me that I could not hold both grief and the vigilant protection of my family in the same place at the same time.

This forced me to live a very split life, battling between my two biggest priorities. The desire—and need—to focus on processing my grief remained strong and continued with counseling. When I was with my family and in therapy, I found pockets of time to incorporate my grief work with Alissa and my girls. At home I felt more loose and could play steamroller with the girls with lots of laughter. Or I would zone out on the couch holding each of them while watching *Shaun the Sheep* together. The times when I was present and open, I felt like I could be me. Then there were quiet moments when Alissa and I held each other and talked openly with each other. Even though this could be painful, I felt safe. Those experiences were beautiful.

In public or at work my guard was up at all times while I tried to remain invisible. I was tense, with my eyes peeled and ears always scanning. If my family was with me, I was on edge, sharp and impatient. Trips to Costco used to be a fun errand but now started to feel like get-in-and-get-out military operations. I didn't want to be recognized or stopped. We cruised the aisles grabbing samples and placing them in the girls' laps with barely a pause. In certain scenarios I began to lose my filter if I noticed an injustice or if I felt I was being taken advantage of and would make comments or complain freely. All of these things were not me, though they were a part of who I was becoming.

Over time these worlds became harder to keep separated. The more they blended, the more my grief and connection with Emilie faded farther back into the recesses of my heart. The loss festered, but I felt embattled. Because of the real emotional and physical danger almost everywhere we went, I had to feverishly watch over what we still had as threats continued to pour in through mail, email, and the door.

Chapter 5

Coping on New Ground

The more insular I became, the harder it was to relate to others. I missed out not only on meaningful connections with other people in my community, but I also missed the opportunity to extend empathy to the other people impacted by what happened at Sandy Hook. It wasn't until Bill Aldenberg, an FBI agent who responded to the shooting at Sandy Hook, took the stand that I understood how profoundly this tragedy impacted so many lives.

Bill carried himself with the full force and respect of the FBI. Despite this feeling of authority about him, he was unpretentious, with a natural humility. He seemed almost uncomfortable, emotional even, while talking with other family members. He kept his voice low and struggled to look us in the eye. He was nervous because we all knew what he was there to do. Bill had firsthand knowledge of what happened the day of the shooting. He didn't want to retraumatize or inflict unnecessary pain on us again. In fact, earlier, our lawyers warned us we might want to wait outside the courtroom during Bill's testimony, but nobody did. After being around him for just a few minutes, I was filled with gratitude that he responded to the school that day.

Conspiracy trolls had used photographs and screenshots from news coverage to argue that Bill, too, was a crisis actor. They followed the same patterns and wrote blog posts and created videos analyzing the way Bill held his weapon—or that his uniform did not look exactly as it should, thereby convincing themselves that the only explanation for such absurdity was that he wasn't an FBI agent at all.

On the stand, Bill described exactly what he saw, exactly what he felt, exactly where the mass shooting occurred. He provided gut-wrenching testimony, leaving no doubt about what really happened. Along the way he naturally debunked many of the conspiracy arguments by answering simple questions.

"Is what you saw in that school fake?" our lawyer Chris asked him.

"No, sir," Bill answered, trying to stifle his emotions.

"Was it *synthetic*?" That last word dripping with disgust.

"No, sir . . . No, sir." The answer came just above a whisper.

"Did you see any actors that day, Bill?" Chris's tone turned sharp.

"No, sir." This time, Bill's fortitude began to crumble. His shoulders slumped. He had to take a few breaths.

This time with sincerity, Chris asked, "Were those children real?"

"It was awful . . . awful . . ." Bill responded, his lips trembling before lowering his head, grasping for composure. Through tears, he continued, "It was awful."

My heart swelled with compassion for what Bill had been through and subtle surprise that I had not truly considered what someone else's experience from that day was like. It wasn't that I was cold, but that I had been so bombarded. Not only did I carry the memories and weight from that day, but so many times, I was forced to listen to and bear someone else's. I had no choice but to tune all of them out.

The person who broke through was, of all people, Peter Lanza, the shooter's father. Around two months after the shooting, Marian Salzman, the amazing public relations person, told me and Alissa that she had a conversation with the public relations group helping the shooter's family in the aftermath of the shooting. She was told that Peter felt as though my comments during the press conference were like an olive branch and that if we wanted to, he would be willing to meet with us.

Alissa and I wondered what could be gained by meeting with the father of the troubled young man who murdered Emilie. My sentiments from the night after the shooting echoed Alissa's—that our hearts did go out to this family, and we couldn't understand how hard this experience must be for them. Those sentiments were even more truthful two months later than they were when I uttered them.

Also, a major part of making grief a priority for us was my and Alissa's desire to learn as much as we could about the details of the shooting and anything else we could from that day. We attended every one of the scores of meetings with law enforcement, town officials, and school administrators but of course there were a lot of questions that remained unanswered. As we contemplated the olive branch being offered, we understood that with the shooter and his mother being gone, Peter was the only person who might be able to shed some light on what we hadn't yet found.

Setting up the meeting was surprisingly fast. Within days, Alissa and I pulled into the parking lot of a generic office building in Wilton, Connecticut. We were nervous and not sure quite what to say or expect. Our intentions were pure, though, and we remained open for whatever might occur. We entered an empty elevator and just as the doors were closing I held them open for someone I saw in the lobby. Alissa shot me a quick and annoyed look as if to say, *Why do you have to be so polite all the time!* She was right. We were nervous and now we had the awkward silence of a third wheel elevator ride.

Until the stranger turned to me and said, "I really want to thank you for being willing to speak with me." I couldn't believe it, but I had held the doors open for Peter Lanza. This was awkward.

Peter was a tall, middle-aged man with a soft countenance. The awkwardness between the three of us surprisingly did not last long. We exchanged our condolences and the understanding that we were all parents grieving our children. Quickly, Alissa and I were able to articulate that one reason we wanted to meet was to encourage him to cooperate with authorities and release any pertinent medical, mental health, or other information. Peter had refused to give any interviews or do anything publicly out of respect to the victims and their families. We started to explain that he had the power to help find answers when he anxiously interrupted us. "I already am," he said reassuringly, then described his sincere desire to "find out why this all happened and will do anything I can to help."

After that, it felt that something else opened up with Peter and he began to explain some family history. How after he and his first wife, Nancy, divorced he moved to a nearby town but continued to support her and their two sons both financially and emotionally as much as possible. He spoke of playing Legos and going on hikes with his youngest son, Adam. As his son's mental health declined and he became more isolated, he cut off almost all contact with his father and brother and was only communicating with his mother, with whom he lived, by handwritten notes. Prior to the shooting, though, he hadn't seen or spoken to his son in over two years, despite many phone calls and emails that were never returned.

He opened up about his son's mental health challenges and the medications he was given. After he and Nancy took him to specialist after specialist, he was eventually removed from Newtown public schools and became homeschooled. He grew more and more isolated, and although Peter knew something was wrong, there was no way for him to see the signs of what was to come.

On December 14, 2012, Peter heard about the shooting and left work early when he heard reports that the perpetrator had attended Sandy Hook Elementary School. When he pulled into his driveway, a reporter was waiting for him and told him that someone from his family was involved.

We spent almost two hours talking with Peter, connecting on a deeply human level across what many people would have considered an impassable crevasse. Alissa and I realized that our troubles and his were very different. It was clear to us that he desperately wanted to understand what happened to his son. He wanted to know why he did something so evil, as Peter put it. We both were dealing with misinformation and lies being spread about our children. Though Alissa and I were also buoyed up by those with compassion for what happened to our daughter, while his son was despised. It felt as though Peter was very much alone with what kept him up at night. Which made his willingness to do everything in his power to help provide answers and healing for all of us that much more remarkable.

One evening I was in line waiting to pick up food at a restaurant and struggling to get out of a conversation with a man who suddenly realized we were "one of those families" and that Emilie was "one of the victims." As soon as he started talking, I dreaded what I knew I had to endure in the next few minutes. I listened to him go into detail about how much it hurt to watch all that on the news and how it just got so painful that after a while he had to turn the television off.

It didn't matter how much time had passed, each such occurrence was intensely draining. My muscles would tense up, unbidden, when they told me, "That night I gave my children the biggest hug." I never knew how to respond or what to feel during these encounters.

Although the support was genuine and well-intended, it brought with it another layer of pressure. Every time I filled up gas or went to work it felt as if all eyes were on me. A new fear and panic arose for me to always appear or act a certain way. In those moments when others would share their stories, I felt a responsibility to fully listen, and then put them at ease. It was as if people had forgotten that they gave their child a hug that night while I did not.

In reality, all I wanted was a piece of my old self back, the person I used to be before December 14. I wanted his worries, his *simplicity*. But there was nothing from my old life, before the tragedy, that could prepare me for what I was encountering in my new one. Every entity I had been dealing with since that day, whether it was grief, the media, conspiracists, or loving people with good intentions, added another layer of complexity that enveloped my new life.

With each passing month after the shooting, I had withdrawn further into a cocoon. I slowly stopped connecting with others and developed severe social anxiety. I kept my head down and avoided eye contact. Every layer weighed heavily on my shoulders. The depression blocked out all light and color. My new life in this new post–Sandy Hook world was dark and lonely.

Among the mayhem caused by every outside influence, my family worked hard internally to establish a routine while figuring out our "new normal." We didn't hide from our grief, but we also tried to engage in regular activities with the girls like going to the movies or the zoo. It was important for us to help them imprint on their individuality and sense of self while dealing with our individual pain or triggers from Emilie's death. Part of that routine was engaging in grief therapy. Almost every Sunday we met with a small group of other Sandy Hook families at a place called Healing Hearts. Here, Madeline and Samantha were able to meet with special counselors and play with other siblings. While in another plain meeting room Alissa and I went with our own counselors and other parents. I had never participated in any type of group therapy before and was initially determined to stay back and remain quiet. So it came as a shock to me that after hearing a few parents break the ice and share, I felt the urge to do the same. We quickly were able to connect with other parents, forming bonds and friendships. In that room, with those people, I didn't feel the pressure I did everywhere else. We didn't even have to talk to feel heard or understood.

On one particular Sunday, I wasn't able to shed my dark layers off at the door. I felt closed off and disconnected. For the first half hour, I sat like a lump. Until one mother shared a story about seeing her son's favorite brand of peanut butter at the grocery store that week. She told us that she became so overwhelmed that she had to abandon her cart right in the middle of the aisle and go home. Her son apparently loved peanut butter to the point of it becoming a nuisance. She'd unearth spoons with peanut butter residue in places where there shouldn't be spoons. Then one day she couldn't find her son anywhere. Everyone was looking all over the house and no sign of him. "Finally," she said, while smiling, crying and laughing, "we found him behind the couch, fast asleep, holding a spoon of peanut butter in his mouth!"

Her story totally broke the room. Together, we laughed. We all knew exactly how that felt in our own way. At Healing Hearts I felt like the children who went through the wardrobe into Narnia. It was another existence I could experience outside of the world I was living in.

Early in my personal work with Deb there was some progress as well, albeit slow and sporadic. It felt good when I could focus on something that was helpful and hopeful. Implementing what I learned in therapy into this new world I was in felt stimulating. By the early summer of 2013, however, any momentum I had gained came to a grinding halt. The desire to tackle grief head-on had almost entirely disappeared. The tools we worked on just a few weeks earlier no longer seemed to have the same effect as they did initially. I grew frustrated and felt stagnant, and became irritated with everyone and everything everywhere I went.

I was in line at the grocery store checkout trying not to notice all the green and white 12/14/12 stickers everywhere. The lady in front of me was complaining to her friend about how her son wasn't given a pair of the specialty sneakers Nike had produced in the Sandy Hook school colors, green and white. The shoes were delivered with no plan with how they should be distributed. Apparently this woman's son missed out on the free giveaway and was really upset. I kept my head down, like always, and tried to ignore her. I worked even harder not to just yell, "My daughter didn't die so your kid could get free shoes, lady!" Instead, like our friend, I set my few items down and walked out of the store.

After repeating this story to Deb, I told her it left me feeling stuck.

"What do you mean by stuck?"

Slowly but surely I watched Alissa and the other parents begin to adjust to their new normal. It wasn't a straightforward upward journey, but it seemed they were making progress while my momentum appeared to vanish. The tools and tactics I learned in therapy no longer had the same effects as they did before. I told her how the moments when I worked on grief before helped me feel connected to something but when I was among the rest of the world I felt out of place. Now every interaction with myself, grief, or with others had become subdued and flat. Everything appeared gray, as if the color all around and inside of me had been sucked away. Even if something from our therapy came up for me to work on, my body just stopped responding.

"Interesting." Deb thought for a moment. "What else?"

"That's the thing, I don't *feel* anything else. It doesn't feel like depression, or at least how I understand depression. It just feels flat, like . . . nothing."

"Robbie," Deb began softly, speaking like someone who gingerly steps onto a frozen lake, testing its fortitude, "is there anything from your past that you think needs to be resolved but hasn't been?"

That question somehow triggered an emotion to emerge. It was dim at first, barely perceptible in its flickers, while also unmistakable. Somehow, subconsciously, I knew what it was without even knowing it had been there. The emotion began to rise up from the deepest part of my being, growing in light and presence. Until I stopped it.

"Yes," was all I could answer.

Deb stayed still and quiet, allowing the uncomfortable feeling to rest long enough until I acclimated to it.

"Well, you see," I began, surprised by the sound of my own voice, "there was some sexual abuse in my family when I was a child." Then I caught myself. I cleared my throat quickly and tried to recover. "But that was a long time ago, and I've gotten over it."

Deb's eyes continued to be steady and compassionate. "You know, I can't help but wonder if, maybe, some of those emotions from your childhood may be impacting the way your body and thoughts are responding to your grief work?"

"What do you mean?" I asked, genuinely confused. "They don't have anything to do with each other." *How could my childhood abuse have a single thing to do with grieving Emilie?*

"That may seem true," Deb pressed, "but as we've said before, if you resist an emotion, it will persist, right?"

"Right."

"Well, if we have unresolved issues from our past, they don't go away, and they will persist . . . into everything, especially and naturally seeping into areas of great pain and trauma."

I sat there, flummoxed. This was such an uncomfortable concept for me to wrap my head around. As Deb and I continued to work through the session, however, the emotion that ignited after her question became bigger, brighter, and clearer until I couldn't ignore it. If I was to continue healing from trauma and grief as an adult, brought on from Emilie's death, I would have to address the trauma and abuse I suffered as a child. That was an extremely daunting realization for me. I had pushed all of this down for a reason.

The reality was that I had been sexually abused by a family friend at age six. His name was Douglas Stoddard, and he was also our Mormon bishop. Unknown to me at the time, he also sexually assaulted my three brothers. And if all of that wasn't horrible enough, I found out later that my father, who had also been in church leadership, sexually molested my sister. All of this occurred before I entered into the second grade, and it shattered me.

I'd grown up as the fourth of five children in a home constantly filled with chaos. My family was not well equipped at emotional expression or regulation. That dynamic, combined with the pressure of being raised in a high-demand religion, where obedience was directly correlated to worthiness for God and my own personal value, made it hard and unnatural for me to ever feel seen or heard.

Disagreements in my family were usually addressed loudly and I realized that, for me, remaining quiet and unseen generally worked in my favor. I avoided conflicts and never developed my voice for myself. Rather, I stood in the role of a peacekeeper whenever possible.

I formed a deep resistance to showing any real, emotional vulnerability. Expressing genuine emotion left me feeling exposed to ridicule or, worse yet, was used as ammunition for others to later exploit me. This, coupled with my tendency for silence, left me defenseless when I was sexually abused.

Naturally, I responded to that abuse exactly as I had been trained—that my voice didn't matter. So, as that hurt child, I shoved the abuse as deep as I possibly could, then created the best labyrinth my childhood mind could create to protect me from ever accessing it. Afterward, I promised that I would *never* allow anyone to have power over me like that again; then I tried to live my life as though nothing happened.

Even though the abuse against me and all of my siblings eventually came to light, I was already adamant that I wouldn't let the abuse define or affect me in any way. As a result, I stayed silent at times when I needed to be heard, causing a counterfeit voice to develop in place of my authentic self. Through ongoing therapy, I eventually came to realize I had developed coping strategies that usually fell into the realms of "Out-fun. Out-wit. Out-run." The more fun I piled into my life, the more it would bury my bad experiences. When needed, a quick wit could be used to advantageously wriggle out of any trouble. When all else failed, I developed a knack of running from every perceived physical or emotional threat.

As time went on, I saw this pattern of behavior repeat itself many times throughout my life. Even though I was becoming aware of it, it still reared its ugly head, especially in how I responded to Alex Jones and his conspiracy cronies. The megaliths atop the social media empires, who had much more to gain from Jones's millions of followers and views, quickly reconfirmed that my voice didn't matter—as they consistently chose to protect *his* content on their platforms over the safety of my family.

There was no way I could "out-fun" the conspiracy world, knowing what they could do if I ever dared try to smile or laugh publicly ever again. I couldn't "out-wit" a group of people that succumbed to illogical lies and believed their own made-up contradictory theories. There was no way to "out-run" a large group of people hidden among us that mostly stayed anonymous. No matter how hard I tried.

When a group of Sandy Hook parents sued the gun manufacturer Remington, I declined to join the suit. I saw what the hecklers did to the Sandy Hook father when he had the wherewithal to speak about the impacts of gun violence. I'd already been eviscerated in the media. I also didn't want to give any credence or validation to the false notion that I was out trying to take away people's guns. In addition, I was extremely fearful of what could befall my family if I were to ever speak out. I felt the best way to protect my family, including Emilie's five- and four-year-old sisters, was to resort to the same tactics that saved me as a child—which was to keep quiet, not engage, and hope eventually they would stop.

New armor arose from my previous coping strategies—"*Outgood.*" Maybe if we just stayed quiet, focused on our work, and did not engage, they might forget and leave us alone. Alissa and Joey's mom, Michele Gay, teamed up and started *Safe and Sound Schools*, a non-profit focused on school safety with an emphasis on crisis prevention, response, and recovery. They purposefully stepped outside of the gun rights vs. control debate, wanting to make a real difference in the safety of every school, every student, every day. Alissa and I also cofounded *The Emilie Parker Art Connection*, a non-profit designed to honor Emilie and her love of art by connecting children suffering from trauma, abuse, and neglect to the power of art therapy. The money we raised was donated to wonderful organizations that promoted those ideals. It was a beautiful way to reinforce and aid our pursuit of healing.

Just because we were not engaging directly against Alex Jones and his ilk didn't mean that we were going to passively sit and allow them to completely walk all over us. But my hope that focusing on ourselves and our important work while ignoring the conspiracists was the best way to keep Emilie's memory alive could not have been more wrong.

Since the morning Emilie had been killed, we had all been in a constant fight-or-flight response. It seemed that we never got a break from any internal or external stressor. Whether that was from the initial shock that our daughter was murdered, to Alex Jones and conspiracists, threats and meetings with FBI agents, the guilt Alissa and I shared over failing to protect Emilie, and constantly worrying if we were handling grief correctly with ourselves and our daughters. These and many other issues felt like spinning plates we were trying to keep upright, constantly racing around to attend to each one before they fell. Now, my job situation added another plate into the mix.

In the summer of 2013, I was home alone and received an email from my work informing me that they would be changing the work schedule and establishing a new staffing model. But only for our unit. Before even finishing the email, I slammed my hand against the desk and yelled, "I can't believe it!" The biggest reason Alissa and I had decided I would take this job was because they offered twenty-four-hour shifts. Being able to work twenty-four-hour shifts meant I never had to work back-to-back days and was only required to work eight to ten days a month. This allowed me to spend more time at home with my young family. With days between shifts, I never felt burned out or dreaded going into work. Besides, both of our families lived out West and I had no other reason to bring my family across the country to take a job back East if not for this particular schedule.

We had spent the previous six years working and going to school while simultaneously starting and growing our family. All that work, all that sacrifice, was for this: to finally have a job that could support us and let me be home more. In my mind we moved to Newtown, Connecticut, for this company. We enrolled Emilie at Sandy Hook Elementary for this company. And she was killed because of it. Now, five months later, how dare they try to take away my twenty-four-hour shifts.

I read the email again, only to become more outraged. This time all the words I was thinking came pouring out as I screamed, kicked, and threw things. I felt 100 percent justified for my outburst and used my anger to fuel a vehement response back to upper management telling them I was not going to comply.

When Alissa came home, I showed her the email and she read my response. This wasn't the first time I had reacted emotionally to an email from work. She worried that sooner or later my grace period for such a reaction would evaporate and I could lose my job. A big part of me knew she was right, but I wouldn't feel that until later. Right then I just wanted to feel justified for standing up for myself.

Deep down I didn't like feeling angry or responding like this. I knew it wasn't the real me. I was scared and I still didn't know why or how to admit it.

BY LATE SUMMER OF 2013, my family was in dire need of a break. And again, my friend Jake from PA school provided one. Jake and his fiancée Kristina's wedding arrived just when my family needed to get as far away from Sandy Hook as possible. We were so happy for the couple, but much like everything else in our lives now, the trip was met with trepidation.

Back in PA school Jake always felt right at home with our family. He, too, came from a large family and was comfortable around our children who loved him like an uncle. Emilie, being the oldest, especially benefited from their friendship, filled with hide-and-seek, jokes, and good, old-fashioned talking.

The previous summer, in 2012, Jake and Kristina had visited us in Connecticut so Kristina could meet the family. She was enthusiastically embraced by all. One evening during their stay, the conversation about their wedding came up. Emilie, as was her custom, stopped what she was doing to join the adult conversation. After a few minutes of talk about who would get to do what during the ceremony, Emilie offered her opinion.

"I'll be your flower girl; I would love that!" Problem solved. It was so funny to me how hilarious and awkward Emilie's contribution was for everyone. Jake and Kristina shared quick glances with each other, silently battling over who would break the news to Emilie, until Kristina stepped in with a quick save. She told Emilie that was a great idea, but they would have to talk about it some more.

"We'll put you on the list," she said.

Satisfied with her answer, Emilie went downstairs. Later, Alissa found Emilie in her closet and asked what she was up to.

"I wanted to show Kristina the dress I could wear if they chose me to be the flower girl." Emilie turned to Alissa holding her favorite and very pretty, very white dress. Alissa came back upstairs giggling in such a contagious way, we all fell into fits of laughter before she could even get the story of Emilie's antics out. When I say Emilie can light up a room, these are the moments I'm talking about.

When Emilie came back upstairs, without the dress, Kristina asked her, "Emilie, did you know, at weddings, white dresses are reserved only for the brides?"

"No way, really?" Emilie said, unaware that Alissa had ratted her out.

"Yes, really! So that means whoever the flower girl is will get a brand-new dress that they'll get to keep."

"Really!"

"Really," Kristina answered, then added, "I promise."

NOW, A YEAR LATER, Alissa and I were nervous about returning to the Pacific Northwest for Jake and Kristina's wedding. That area held a very special place in our hearts. It was the place where so many friendships were made, where Samantha was born, and we felt our family was finally whole and complete. Those feelings and memories hadn't yet been infiltrated with grief and trauma. It was a place where our "old lives" were still protected. Yet, how would the Pacific Northwest look and feel now, without Emilie there with us?

Those anxieties were fresh on my mind when the plane landed in Portland, Oregon. I grabbed Alissa's hand tightly as we drove from the airport toward the memories of our old life. We both braced ourselves to be overwhelmed with grief, just like so many times before, watching precious memories wilt from the writhing pain felt by Emilie's absence. But those feelings didn't come.

Instead, miraculously, as we drove through Portland, Alissa and I both felt Emilie *with* us! She was here, among the towering trees, luscious foliage, and flowing rivers. Memories here didn't hurt the way we had anticipated. We could see and feel her in everything and everywhere. In awe, we glanced at each other wordlessly, with joyful tears in our eyes.

"Madeline, Samantha, look over there. Do you remember that place?"

"That's OMSI!" Madeline's face lit up with memories of her own of the Oregon Museum of Science and Industry, "We used to play in the water there with Emilie!"

These encounters replayed a number of times in their own versions as we passed more familiar places like the Oregon Zoo and the Rose Gardens. The memories and places we had been dreading brought Emilie back to us instead. It was so beautiful to feel the car full of Emilie, instead of the heavy, dark cloud we'd been living in for months. Eventually, we turned north and drove over the Columbia River into Washington State on our way to meet Jake and Kristina in Seattle.

DURING THE BIG WELCOME BARBECUE that evening, it became apparent that even feeling Emilie's presence couldn't totally release me from the continuing emotional work that followed me everywhere. Although I was making headway in therapy in terms of understanding myself, my stuck emotions persisted. Too often, this made it hard for me to raise my head and engage with new people. This was supposed to be when friends and family, who were spread across both coasts, mixed and mingled, but I struggled to make conversation. Though I was surrounded by the unique beauty of Puget Sound, I was unable to see or feel the vibrant colors around me. I was frustrated that even here, among warm people and filled with a powerful experience from earlier that morning, I still desperately wanted to withdraw into my cocoon of illusional safety.

I pulled Alissa aside and told her how I was feeling. It came as no surprise, then, when I volunteered to go to a grocery store to replenish some snacks and drinks. I needed a reprieve from the social pressure to try and emotionally reset. Although my therapy tools hadn't been working, it didn't stop me from trying.

At the store I was having trouble locating a certain item when someone started to approach me. I froze reflexively, put my head down, and purposefully avoided eye contact. I came here for a reprieve from any kind of interaction and just wanted to be left alone. As the person got closer, I turned my shoulder to express that I did not want to be addressed in any form. I feared an awkward encounter from a thoughtful well-wisher, but braced myself for something worse as they stopped right next to me in the empty aisle and spoke: "Is there anything I can help you find?" It was only a store clerk, and all my anxiety was for nothing, but I still remained frozen.

Looking down at his shoes, for what felt like an extraordinary amount of time, a thought came over me: *Look up.* I hesitated and the thought returned. *Look up . . . breathe . . . it's okay.*

I slowly lifted my head, stopping halfway when I noticed the man's green apron. It was a gorgeous deep forest green, amplified against a stunningly simple white T-shirt. My head raised fully and met his eyes. My body suddenly relaxed and I felt safe asking him for what I needed. It was the first time I had experienced *color* in a long time. With my head fully raised, I looked all around and noticed loud pops of color practically screaming at me. Bright orange, red, and blue boxes and packages were all vying for attention like dogs at a pound begging to be picked up. It was a vibrant sensation in my new world that felt almost familiar. After I purchased what was needed and made my way out to the rental car, I wondered if I was capable of allowing that light and color to penetrate through the dark layers that were surrounding my new life.

It was as if something within me had awakened. It was simple but I made a choice that contradicted my fear. *Look up, it's okay.* And it was okay. In that particular moment, it was okay for me to choose something other than the primal response I had grown accustomed to. In deep gratitude and growing appreciation, I rolled down all the windows and soaked in the smells from the salty shore and absorbed the deep blue water, the towering white peaks, and the thick green forests surrounding me. Across the country from Sandy Hook, I felt a peace I hadn't experienced since this new life started. I let it surround me, and the renewed experience of light and color allowed me to enjoy Jake and Kristina's wedding festivities as much as I possibly could. Especially when I watched Madeline and Samantha walk down the aisle, in their off-white dresses with green bows in honor of Emilie, joyfully spreading colorful flower petals ahead of the bride and groom.

Following the wedding, we were able to meet for a family reunion with Alissa's family down on the Oregon coast. While in the area, we visited a clinic I worked at during my PA training. During that visit, the medical director offered me a job, if I was interested in coming back. Later during our trip we continued to visit with friends, and I met up with other colleagues from PA school where I received another job offer to teach at my alma mater and was told about another job opening in a NICU. Three job opportunities in three days caught us completely off guard.

Still, it forced us to ask, "Are we ready to leave Sandy Hook?" And the biggest question of all, "Should we?"

Not only did I feel more of Emilie's enduring presence around us during the entire trip, color continued to captivate me and emotions sifted through as we contemplated what was next for us. More importantly, though, I was making progress.

Chapter 6
The Spoils of Lies

As the trial progressed, Alissa and I were learning so much more about the other parents and their children by way of our extended time with one another and their testimonies on the stand. Nicole Hockley spoke about her son Dylan and his distaste for vitamins. Dylan was autistic and very sensitive to different stimulations, especially taste. She and Ian at the time had been working with Dylan every morning trying to make taking his vitamins easier. She tearfully testified how, on the morning of the shooting, Dylan took his vitamins by himself with no fuss and she was so proud of him. I learned that Jennifer Hensel liked to read poetry and how that had helped her in her grieving process. She wasn't aware that I had written a whole story in rhyme as a way to process my feelings, which she asked me to share with her.

And on a walk with Ian Hockley, after I unconsciously reached down and plucked a dandelion out of a flower bed, I told him about how when Emilie was really little, she loved picking flowers. So much, in fact, that it became a nuisance because if we took our eyes off her for even a second she would pluck someone's garden down like a goat.

Even after a few conversations with Emilie, the temptation of something so pretty was hard to resist and she'd fall off the wagon and start picking again. Finally, one day, I told Emilie that some flowers are only for looking and some flowers are perfect picking flowers. Then I showed her a dandelion and told her she could always pick as many of these flowers as she wanted, and it would never bother anyone. The plan both worked and backfired. We didn't have to worry about her picking other people's flowers as much, but we started finding yellow dandelions everywhere in our house, our cars, even in her bed.

All these interactions were such a needed healthy reprieve from the heavy, painful, and emotional demands occurring inside the courtroom. Like the peanut butter story at Healing Hearts, opening up to one another about our children and our personal lives brought us an immense amount of healing. We got to know one another beyond those first, warped impressions formed in the weeks after the shooting. I learned that Dave and Francine Wheeler were light, jovial, and witty. Francine and I learned that we had both told short stories onstage with an international storytelling organization called The Moth. Francine, in turn, told a group of people during lunch, "I didn't know Robbie was . . . funny."

Being able to just let loose and be ourselves with each other was something I didn't expect, but cherished deeply. Our newfound intimacy made it that much more difficult to listen to testimonies as the trial progressed and we learned just how targeted and coordinated Jones's attacks on us were.

Aside from the deeper personal connections being forged between Alissa and myself with the other families, I also developed an increasing emotional connection with the members of our legal team. For over four years, I had admired and was grateful for their expertise and passion for their work. As the trial commenced, though, it became abundantly clear how much everyone involved genuinely cared about this case and, more importantly, all of us. During the trial, we stayed at the same hotel where I watched them work tirelessly into the night, sometimes surviving on granola bars, M&M's, and Bai drinks.

Our team consisted of four main lawyers, along with their staff. Josh Koskoff is bright, discerning, and a much more jovial person than one might expect from someone whose name carries the legacy of the law firm his grandfather established in 1936. Josh was always very involved in the case but also delegated most of the heavy lifting to Chris Mattei, Alinor Sterling, and Matthew Blumenthal. Alinor is a legal sniper whose written motions and arguments are deadly in ways the opposition never sees coming—a talent that Remington Firearms and Norm Pattis learned the hard way. Matthew may have been the most junior member on the team, but he authored the lawsuit against Alex Jones so well that our team won multiple rulings and appeals against every legal challenge brought against it. It may be Josh's last name on the building, but a good leader puts the right people in the right places at the right time. Josh is a good leader and Chris, Alinor, Matt, and their teams were the right people.

One morning, before the court proceedings started, Norm Pattis was sitting with another one of Jones's attorneys from Texas, Andino Reynal, when he realized that Alinor was not in the courtroom. I watched Pattis lean over to Reynal and whisper, "I wonder where Alinor is? I get worried when she isn't around because that usually means she's filing a motion that I'll have to spend three hours working on tonight."

On this particular morning, though, Alinor wasn't writing or filing anything with the court, but was making sure that our expert witness had safely arrived and was ready to testify that day.

Clint Watts, a former FBI agent turned investigative consultant, turned the courtroom into a classroom as he broke down Jones's well-oiled tactics. With the skills Watts garnered throughout his career, studying and investigating how terrorist organizations, foreign governments, and individuals use the internet and social media to spread misinformation and influence behavior, he was a powerful and reliable expert witness.

On the stand he skillfully analyzed video segments of Alex Jones speaking on *Infowars,* calling out how his tactics, personality, and the production methods of his show propagate misinformation and radicalize his audience—mimicking methods used by Al Qaeda. Watts then broke down for the jury the now familiar clip of Jones, just hours after the shooting at Sandy Hook, prophesying on air, "They are coming. They are coming. They are coming."

Josh Koskoff questioned Mr. Watts. "Can you tell us what, if anything, Alex Jones is employing here in regards to the message?" he asked Watts.

"It is fear, over loss of weapons, which he uses as the justification. He stokes anger by repeating it was some sort of a plot. He uses demonization by picking the target for his message as in what the perpetrator is or the existential threat to what they are behind, which, in this case, he says is taking weapons."

Josh follows up and asks, "He talks about 'they' . . . 'they' are coming, 'they' are coming . . . What is the significance of that in terms of its influence on an audience?"

Watts replied simply, "It characterizes . . . the situation as two parties—*us* vs. *them*. That there is some sort of pending or current conflict that is underway."

I SAT COMPLETELY FIXATED and stunned by what Watts was describing. In this one setting, my viewpoint of what had been happening to my family rose from sea level to 10,000 feet. From my day-to-day perspective, Alex Jones appeared to have no rhyme or reason to what he was saying or doing. He flew by the seat of his pants. Yet, this demonstrated that *everything* was systematically set up. The message, his natural gift of gab and bombastic personality, the graphics and production in the video, and the purposeful infrastructure were all coordinated into this well-oiled machine that was specifically designed for this exact situation.

Knowing this video was produced specifically to incite his millions of followers, while victims still were lying where they died inside of Sandy Hook Elementary, hit me with a refined level of horror. I hadn't just inadvertently wandered into Alex Jones's crosshairs.

I was stalked, then ambushed, all according to plan.

Sitting on those hard pews, looking down from this new ten-thousand-foot perspective suddenly gave me vertigo. The realization of what I had actually been up against without knowing the extent of it felt disorienting. My understanding transformed from believing I was dealing with one rattlesnake coiled at my feet to realizing that I was in a field surrounded by thousands of rattlesnakes that Alex Jones had gathered . . . and groomed.

As Watts then made clear, Jones groomed his audience so they were desperate and eager to purchase his products. Every segment of *The Alex Jones Show* is followed with product placement. The products are not from sponsors. Nope. All are items that he supplies and sells himself—creating the need, dilemma, and offering the solution for sale all at once. Many times after demonizing me and trampling on Emilie's memory, he would callously segue into pitching male enhancement pills or special toxicity removal iodine drops. The clip being shown in the courtroom was no different.

What made this so filthy was that every bit was specifically designed and produced in a way that harmed innocent lives. And for what? To enrage his audience to believe there was always an existential threat lurking, ready to come get you? That your water was poisoned, so you'd buy iodine drops? That if you wanted to learn about the "real truth" behind the Sandy Hook plot that he just made up as soon as the shooting happened, you could buy his magazine?

But regardless of how reprehensible I found his methods, Jones's tactics worked. The *Infowars* audience grew from forty-nine million to seventy-three million in the year after the Sandy Hook shooting.

On September 24, 2014, when *Infowars* published an article with the headline "FBI Says No One Killed at Sandy Hook" (which Jones's staff later admitted to publishing with fabricated information in order to pin blame on another party), the website's store brought in $48,229. Within twenty-four hours, as the article was shared across social media, their revenue quintupled to $232,825 on September 25; $128,854 on September 26, before going back to baseline on September 28, at $49,227. The two days that article heavily circulated online brought in over a week's worth of income for *Infowars*—more than a third of a million dollars from just one lie about Sandy Hook.

Through text messages and emails, it was proven that Alex Jones meticulously followed sales numbers day by day—if not hour by hour. Even his own father, David Jones, admitted in a sworn deposition that when they saw spikes in sales, they found out what Alex Jones said on air that day so they could emulate those spikes in the future.

The most staggering number that Watts shared that afternoon was in regard to Alex Jones's online influence. Watts's deep investigative work successfully cleared all the hurdles put in place by Jones and social media companies to prove that between 2012 and 2018, Alex Jones's specific lies about Sandy Hook alone, at a bare minimum, brought over 550 million unique redirects to *Infowars*'s website via social media. I had to wrap my head around that: over 550 million times, someone made the decision to click a link from social media to specifically ingest Alex Jones's fearmongering, demonizing lies about Sandy Hook.

The only thing more jarring than hearing the staggering number of followers and shocking profits Jones cultivated was knowing what these numbers meant to us in the real world. All of the parents and family members on that bench had come in contact with *Infowars* diehards not just online, but in person. They threatened us and jeopardized our physical safety all in the name of Jones's conspiratorial reign of justice. They acted just as they were trained to do.

We knew that one of the persons ingesting the tripe pouring out from *Infowars* was a man named Matthew Mills. This man had previously been arrested after he stormed the 2014 Super Bowl postgame press conference to spew 9/11 conspiracy theories. After the Super Bowl stunt, Alex Jones invited Mills onto his show and praised him as "the man of the hour" and "a guy with real courage" before he offered him a job as a correspondent for *Infowars* "because you've got the right stuff and we salute you . . . anything you need, soldier!"

In 2015, the family of slain Sandy Hook first-grade teacher Victoria Soto, who died shielding her students, were holding their annual 5K charity run. Victoria's sister Jillian testified during our trial that while standing at the finish line with her two young cousins, Mills approached her, wearing a "Team Vicki" T-shirt.

"Are you Jillian Soto?" he asked calmly.

"Yes . . ." Jillian answered the person she had never met before.

Mills then took his phone out and began recording their interaction while shoving a picture of Vicki in Jillian's face, demanding to know why she claimed Vicki was dead. In a panic, Jillian quickly ordered her young cousins to run toward safety, toward family members. Mills continued his harassment, telling her that "Vicki never existed" and claiming that "the Sandy Hook shooting never happened." His harassment continued until the police arrived, when he tried to run away but was quickly apprehended and arrested.

Another known fan of Alex Jones was arrested in Florida after she made a number of threatening phone calls to the parents of a child killed at Sandy Hook. Lucy Richards of Tampa admitted to leaving messages stating, "Death is coming to you real soon. LOOK BEHIND YOU; IT IS DEATH!" Richards eventually served five months in prison and five months of home confinement for her actions. Upon her release, the judge ordered that her internet activity would be monitored, and she was not allowed on *Infowars*'s website or to have any affiliation with material produced by Alex Jones.

In Newtown, one of the most well-known conspiracists was a former school administrator, former highway patrolman, and self-proclaimed school safety expert, Wolfgang Halbig. Originally from Florida, Mr. Halbig at one time offered his school safety expertise to Newtown after the shooting. When his offer was rebuffed, Mr. Halbig began "looking into Sandy Hook," and through his absorption with Alex Jones, became convinced the shooting was fake. It was then he became an outspoken aggressor.

Halbig traveled many times from Florida to Newtown to attend city council and school board meetings, where he demanded he be given evidence and documents to prove the shooting happened. His favorite demand was for receipts for the portable toilets he saw in news coverage the week of the shooting, convinced the presence of portable toilets was proof that the event was staged and planned in advance. Halbig's disturbances during these meetings were extremely cruel, as he demanded that families release death certificates and exhume bodies to prove *our* claims that our children were killed.

Everything got worse when Alex Jones became involved.

Halbig became a regular guest on *Infowars* where he and Alex rode the merry-go-round of disinformation together, confirming one another's lies to themselves. However, in doing so, Jones raised Halbig's clout in conspiracy circles. Jones began sending camera crews with Halbig to these meetings in Newtown, and helped him raise money for travel and other expenses. Jones allowed Halbig on his show, without ever checking his over-embellished résumé.

One such example was that Halbig had spent a year as a Florida state trooper, from 1974 to 1975. Which he later inflated to homicide investigator. In an appeal to the NAACP seeking justice for arrested conspiracist Jonathan Reich—seemingly cc'd to every African American leader whose email Halbig could find, including Dean Baquet, executive editor of the *New York Times*—Halbig said he had driven Martin Luther King Jr. in a protective motorcade. That duty, he wrote, was "the greatest honor this old man of seventy ever had." Indeed it would have been, had King not been assassinated in 1968, six years before Halbig joined the police.

Halbig was also notorious for sending incessant emails to victims' families while cc'ing extended family members, local and national government officials, law enforcement, famous media personalities, and school personnel. His emails to me, which also went to my siblings, in-laws, nieces, and nephews, were littered with pictures of the "real Emilie Parker" and birth certificates "proving" that Alissa and I were not Emilie's parents but rather she was the offspring of Alissa's sister Jill and my little brother, James.

Halbig was also named as a defendant in the lawsuit against Alex Jones and *Infowars*. Even as a defendant, he called my and Alissa's cell phones multiple times, leaving voicemails asking us to "clarify some of the concerns I have." In a new kind of disturbing voicemail, he told Alissa, "I'm reaching out on behalf of Emilie. You need to protect her. I know you know what I'm talking about. To find out that Robbie is not the real father . . . you need to come clean; you need to become the mother you should be because you know what's going on."

Thankfully, after years of torment, sheriff's deputies arrested Wolfgang Halbig in January 2020 for unlawful possession of personal identification, after he emailed victims' family members' social security numbers, phone numbers, addresses, and other delicate personal information to a long list of recipients including "multiple different law enforcement agencies and news stations."

The propagation and rise of conspiracy theorists in the aftermath of Sandy Hook was a novel phenomenon in 2013. Before social media, conspiracies such as the moon landing being sensationalized as fake had a hard time gaining traction and converting millions of people. Our country witnessed a rise in the months after the shooting, especially how social media was manipulated to rapidly spread disinformation. That's why, when the official investigative report about the Sandy Hook shooting was scheduled to be released by the end of 2013, it was met with grave concern from many family members, including mine.

During that year, scores of Freedom of Information Act (FOIA) requests had been submitted by individuals and organizations for the release of 911 calls, investigative findings, and most disturbing, for the crime scene photos. While the investigation was active, the FOIA requests were unable to proceed. However, with the release date looming, there was a legitimate fear among family members as to what Sandy Hook truthers would do if gory photos of our children were made widely available. We couldn't imagine. After what we'd been through, we didn't want to.

The initial Connecticut FOIA laws from 1975 had rarely been updated by the state legislature and were severely behind the times. These antiquated laws were inadequate in a swiftly evolving, digital world filled with people intent on using the laws for malicious harm, not for ethical transparency as was originally intended. The mere thought of any of our surviving children opening up an email one day filled with bloody crime scene photographs of their deceased siblings caused panic for many families.

With help from our local and state representatives, a large number of Sandy Hook families went to the state capital to lobby for updates to the law. Unfamiliar with the legislative process, I was surprised by how much resistance we initially received. Despite all caucuses and committees claiming compassion for our predicament, many raised concerns with the balance of transparency, protection, and government overreach.

It was also unnerving how many lawmakers themselves were dishonest and manipulative in their interactions with us. "I support you and what you are trying to do here," we heard in almost every meeting we attended. "However, *that* caucus and *that* committee *over there* are not on board." We would then set up a meeting with that caucus and that committee . . . only to hear the same thing from them while they pointed their fingers at the previous caucus we just spoke to.

"No wonder nothing productive ever gets done around here!" I told Alissa after one particularly frustrating meeting.

We ended up spending days at the capital, continuing to help the legislature see how a balance of victims' rights, protection from abuse and trauma, and government accountability was all achievable.

Our fight at the capital was not missed by conspiracy trolls as they rampaged online against us. But with just minutes to spare in the legislative session, we were relieved when our efforts were rewarded with an overwhelming vote to protect photos, film, or digital video images "depicting the victim of a homicide." Under the new law, the burden fell on petitioners to show that public interests outweigh the privacy harms to the victim's families.

This win at the capital was a tremendous relief for us and every other family now protected in Connecticut. Unfortunately, in 2013, it also highlighted a growing trend I wished I could get away from. The consistent daily battles forced upon us, both large and small, were met with internal havoc. Every time we put energy into "good" things (like protective legislation), there was always a heavy emotional price tag—even when it was worth it.

Experiences like the FOIA lobbying, warnings from the city about when Wolfgang Halbig was in town, and the constant reminders of 12/14/12 visible everywhere we went helped Alissa and I realize we needed a change. Our summer trip to the Pacific Northwest proved to us that life outside of Newtown and our Sandy Hook family was possible.

We struggled with the idea of leaving the support that Sandy Hook and the other families provided. Where else could we go that had a built-in community of love and support like Newtown? We also understood that a fresh start and a place to raise our girls with more anonymity coincided with our healing goals.

It was a tug-o-war, but facing forward to a new future, we accepted the wonderful job offer back in the land of evergreens, volcanoes, beaches, and where at one time, our family was complete and whole.

Alissa and I knew we could never be all of what we were before, but perhaps this was the place that we could focus not just on battles, but on healing.

Chapter 7

How Do You Sleep at Night?

Throughout our marriage, Alissa and I had moved many times, each move progressing us into an exciting new chapter of life and hope. That journey together led us from Utah to Oregon, Washington, Montana, New Mexico, and Connecticut. Still, we had never experienced a *fresh start* move before, moving away from something with a loss instead of forward with hope . . . since hope could not be trusted.

As we prepared to move away from Connecticut, our biggest struggle was how to honor and carry what we lost with us, into whatever a fresh start entailed. With the first anniversary of the shooting approaching, Emilie's absence weighed heavy on all of us. Alissa and I realized how necessary it was to get away from the cold dark of Connecticut over December 14 and take our family somewhere bright, warm, and tropical, just the four of us.

It bothered me that I had spent so much of that first year dealing with the aftermath of Emilie's death, and not enough time remembering Emilie for who she was when she was alive. I didn't know what the right way to grieve was or how I should be feeling almost a year after her death, but I did know that living my life in fear wasn't it. I wanted time to reminisce and think about Emilie, to share stories of her with Alissa and the girls, but with everything going on at home it was nearly impossible. Thankfully, the warm island breeze provided a helpful reprieve, which allowed me to think about Emilie . . . a lot.

I used to joke that Emilie would make a great play-by-play announcer. Her mind was always firing at the pace of hummingbird wings. Her brain and mouth were so intimately connected that you were constantly getting a current status report about anything that was in her head. By nature, she was very pleasant, personified by the fact that her very first word was not *mommy* or *daddy* but *happy*. She instinctively developed personal connections and formed inside jokes with everyone who knew her.

It was very common to hear Emilie say, "Hey, Dad . . ." seemingly out of the blue, to which I would respond, "Yes, Emilie?" with curiosity, never knowing what to expect. Many times, she'd ask me a question or offer up an astute observation. Sometimes I would just be looped into her train of thought, in a non-conversational way, like a kind of mental hug. However, every so often I would get a, "Hey, Dad?"

"Yes, Emilie?"

"WHO LET THE DOGS OUT?" she cried. "WOOF, WOOF, WOOF, WOOF!" followed by the most adorable and contagious giggle. Emilie loved the Baha Men song—and knew that I *detested* it! This is precisely why it was her favorite daddy-daughter inside joke. She was relentless in her humor with me. I missed that. I missed her.

When December 14 arrived during our getaway, it came with a different feel to it. Madeline and Samantha were innocently excited for a fun day in the sun at the seashore. Alissa seemed focused and thoughtful while I felt neutral with a vacant space in my chest, not yet occupied with any emotion.

The girls played in the water and when I joined them, the fun we experienced felt more natural than it had in months. Alissa's sudden focus was on the number of butterflies she was noticing. She even started keeping count.

Over a year earlier in the early summer of 2012, while at a yard sale, Emilie picked out a butterfly garden kit and was excited about having a pet butterfly. Alissa tried to explain that butterflies don't make great pets and after they hatched she would need to set them free. Emilie was sure her butterfly would be different and was convinced she would show it so much love it would want to stay with her. We spent weeks watching the caterpillars grow and form chrysalises. The anticipation was so exciting, the entire family snuck into Emilie's room to check on their progress multiple times a day. When Emilie—with great excitement—announced from her room one afternoon that the butterflies were emerging, we all rushed in and watched. When it was time to set the butterflies free, Emilie pulled Alissa aside and asked, "Do you think at least one butterfly will sit on my finger before it flies away?" Not wanting to dash any hopes, Alissa smiled and said, "You never know."

Emilie cautiously undid the lid and we all watched the butterflies flutter up and away. Madeline and Samantha squealed, jumping up and down, but Emilie was disappointed that not one butterfly landed on her finger. After that, butterflies became Alissa and Emilie's mother-daughter special connection and she appreciated Emilie choosing such a sweet way to say "Hi" to her.

That night we went to a restaurant, and while waiting for our food, we all took turns telling our favorite stories about Emilie. Suddenly, in the midst of one story, a very clear and distinct soundtrack could be heard throughout the restaurant over the speakers.

"WHO LET THE DOGS OUT? WOOF, WOOF, WOOF, WOOF!"

It felt as though the entire restaurant went silent and everyone in my family turned and stared at me. Alissa grinned while Madeline and Samantha giggled. I sat stunned, looking back at all three of them. The song, much to my dismay, played in its entirety.

Then, as it started to fade, we continued our conversation, until "WHO LET THE DOGS OUT? WOOF, WOOF, WOOF, WOOF!" blared over the speakers again. Eyes wide, this time I couldn't help but grin while Alissa, Madeline, and Samantha all sat stunned. Then, to my absolute pleasure, "WHO LET THE DOGS OUT? WOOF, WOOF, WOOF, WOOF!" played for a *third* time. I raised my arms above my head and gave an exasperated, overly dramatic sigh just as I would have if Emilie had sung the song herself, then exclaimed upward, "Okay, I get it!" We laughed uncontrollably as we tried to sing along, none of us knowing any of the other lyrics.

At that moment, right then, the vacant, emotional space in my chest was filled. Hope saw its opportunity and rushed in to show us what a fresh-start move could feel like. Here we were, all of us remembering Emilie, feeling close to her and each other, while carrying the stinging pain from our loss.

Hey, Dad?

Yes, Emilie . . . yes.

With everything we had been through in the last year, I felt that hope could not be trusted. Not after it betrayed us back in the firehouse. The mere thought of allowing hope to ever enter into my heart again seemed dangerous. Now, Emilie allowed hope to return and motivated us in our move back to the Pacific Northwest.

My new job was filled with wonderful coworkers and colleagues. We quickly purchased a home with some property, feeling like we needed space for ourselves. I built a bit of an over-the-top chicken coop so Madeline and Samantha could raise "therapy chickens" as suggested by Deb. So Fancy, Chickaletta, Yellow, and Banana gave the girls something to care for and love, while they worked on mending their broken hearts.

Alissa and I dove into a complete remodel with our "new" house. After so many different moves in our lives, we wanted to make this home absolutely ours. The remodel challenged us creatively as we thought and communicated about other issues outside of grief, conspiracies, and Sandy Hook. This would be our third time remodeling a house, but the biggest project we had undertaken by far. We hired an architect and contractor even though we did as much work as we could ourselves. We dismantled the place down to its floorboards and studs, removed the staircase, and moved walls. This was also the first time we took on a project like this without the help of Alissa's dad, who was always a huge help with our other houses.

Remodels are known to test and challenge some relationships, but the obstacles we faced in this realm brought us closer. With similar tastes in colors, trimmings, lighting, and the like, we remained on the same page more often than not. Over literally hundreds of trips to the dump, Home Depot, and IKEA, we had lively conversations and were able to spend so much time together. Where we differed on certain choices led to spirited debates and compromises without feelings getting hurt. On one outing to pick out all the inside doors, we were wrapping up our order and the salesman actually thanked us. "You guys were so pleasant to work with," he said with a chuckle. "I had a couple in here yesterday with what I would call very different tastes and it became really awkward really fast for me and my staff."

The fresh start brought with it other challenges. It was impossible to completely leave what happened in Sandy Hook behind in Connecticut, but it did offer us a chance to take back and own our story, our narrative, on our terms. So now the question was, what were we going to do with it? How would I respond when meeting new people and they inevitably asked, "How many children do you have?" Who could we trust with our history, and who did we need to be judicious with in sharing that story?

Thankfully, the new school where we enrolled Madeline and Samantha was very accepting of our story. They were also more than happy to hear and implement some updated school safety suggestions. At this school, our daughters were received simply as "new students" and didn't carry the stigma of being "one of the siblings."

The anonymity granted being a world away from Newtown was refreshing and beneficial in many ways, while at other times it could be awkward. My retreat into isolation in Sandy Hook was accepted without much thought. It seemed normal, even understandable. And people in Newtown seemed willing to give me space. But now, in new environments where I was meeting new people almost every day, my social anxiety was magnified.

The uncertainty and fear I felt during our awkward run-ins around town in Connecticut was now doubled. How could I possibly know who to trust? In conversation with my new coworkers and neighbors, I was often confusing and clumsy. I was standoffish and awkward. I asked few details about other people's lives and I offered even fewer about my own. I kept my head down, as if constantly analyzing my shoelaces for perfect symmetry. Fortunately, I could trust and felt comfortable around the friends we'd made when Emilie was still alive. But when I extended myself beyond that circle, I was reminded that Sandy Hook's determined conspiratorial aftermath was no respecter of distance and people. It followed us everywhere we went.

While attending church for the first time, an older gentleman approached me and introduced himself. That morning, Alissa and I had literally practiced what we would say when asked about our children, so when his inevitable question came, "How many children do you have?" I was ready with a prepared answer.

"I have three daughters. My oldest would be seven and my other two are six and four years old." Even though it felt a bit rehearsed, I was pleased. We continued to have a superficial, yet affable conversation. After he walked away, I expressed an audible sigh of relief.

I hadn't noticed the other gentleman behind me who walked a few steps over almost immediately and asked, "You said your oldest daughter *would* be seven—did she die?"

Caught somewhat off guard, I responded quickly, "Yes, she passed away a little over a year ago."

"Do you mind if I ask how she died?" he continued, with decidedly more interest than compassion.

It was my first time divulging our story and I stumbled. "Well . . . yeah, um . . . well, we just moved here from Connecticut. My oldest daughter, Emilie, attended Sandy Hook Elementary and was one of the victims in the shooting."

"Oh," he began, pausing briefly. "Well . . . you know, we have a lot of pro–Second Amendment people at this church. I just think that maybe you should know that."

I was so caught off guard and bewildered by his response that I sputtered out, "So?"

He apparently had nothing else to add except for, "Well, it was nice meeting you," before walking away.

I tried to make myself believe that he just didn't know how to respond to the news about Emilie's death, like many people before him. However, I couldn't shake this feeling that he meant exactly what he said. That, at best, he viewed me as some sort of Second Amendment agitator or, at worst, as an existential threat to his way of life merely because my daughter was murdered in a mass shooting.

A few months into my new job, I was up late, performing my weekly ritual of monitoring the internet for new conspiracy material and potential threats. Being away from Newtown lifted some of the angst I felt so heavily while I lived there. I made a solid effort to cut back on how often I actively scanned for material to once a week while at work. This lifted some of the weight I carried constantly but not in a way that triggered my guilt that I wasn't doing enough. Even though most of the fervor of Sandy Hook deniers leveled out after the one-year anniversary, a core base of hoaxers was still active and posting new videos of "research" on YouTube.

Within five months after our move, I found a video that was one of those shared screen tutorials, like you'd see during a college lecture. A young twentysomething, professional-looking female was on one half of the screen, with the document she was sharing on the other. As part of her presentation that she shared with the conspiracy world were county records from the sale of the house we had just moved into and were currently remodeling. Shocked, I watched as she magnified and dictated every detail she could find about the history of the property, paying particular attention to the sale price and highlighting the address a number of times before signing off with, "Good work, everybody, tracking this stuff down. We won't stop—keep up the good work!"

Although our departure away from Newtown made it so the tragedy was no longer in our face everywhere we went, experiences such as these regularly reminded me that the threat to my family's safety remained very real and active. The threats may not have been elevated to full volume all the time, like in Newtown, but they were felt in everything, everywhere, all at once. I could never, ever, let my guard down.

As time passed, we slowly but surely progressed and established a routine that felt comfortable and safe. Back in familiar territory, we regularly visited places like the Portland Rose Gardens and attended their free outdoor concerts. Emilie loved the Rose Gardens even though so many beautiful flowers without being able to pick them drove her crazy as a three-year-old. One time while walking through the many aisles of roses, Alissa turned around and found Emilie holding a gorgeous and very large pink rose. Emilie quickly explained that she didn't pick it but had found it on the ground. We couldn't argue with her logic, but told her it might be best to put the rose in the basket of Madeline's stroller until we got out to the car.

We started to create new memories after we moved back, like exploring lava tunnels on Mount Saint Helens or hiking to dozens of different waterfalls. Both girls started at new schools where they were able to establish their own identities as Madeline and Samantha and not only as Emilie's sister. On a typical overcast afternoon while out for a walk while the girls were in school, Alissa piped up and asked me, "Do you know what I love about these gray Northwest days? It's that it allows the colors around me to pop more vividly." These mixtures of old and new routines for all of us included a tremendous amount of work processing our grief, both individually and as a family.

We began attending the Dougy Center for Grieving Children & Families in Portland, Oregon, a facility focused on child and family grief. Each program was designed for specific needs. Children could belong to a group who had lost a parent, lost a family member to suicide, or, in Madeline and Samantha's case, Tuesday evenings were reserved for children who had lost a sibling. This allowed the girls to interact with other children as grieving peers and playmates. The rooms downstairs designated for children included an art room, game room, theater room, dress-up room, and a big padded room where you could just let it all out. The parents were welcomed to meet together upstairs and share stories and experiences.

Alissa and I also continued our relationship with Deb remotely, which was a huge blessing. As success in our healing progressed, we became more comfortable sharing our story as we saw fit for us. After a school choir performance the girls participated in, I was standing on the other side of the gym watching Alissa talk with another mom we had become acquaintances with. All of a sudden I watched the mom place both hands over her mouth, then reach out and hug Alissa reassuringly. I smiled, as that was a classic sign Alissa had told her our story as it came up naturally in their conversation. When Alissa came over to me, I stated, "So she knows now, huh?" Alissa sighed. "Ya, she knows now. She told me that Madeline had mentioned her sister that died to her and she wanted to know if she handled that situation okay." These types of interactions made us feel hopeful that our work was bearing some fruit we could see and feel.

The conspiracy engine kept humming along, and we continued to receive emails and private messages, and found disturbing videos online. Though I admit these did not feel as imminent as a threat as they had before. There were always new tragedies and new enemies for them to attack and Sandy Hook always seemed to be mentioned, but we had learned what needed more of our attention and what did not.

Feeling more comfortable while still figuring out how to assimilate in our new lives, we were able to engage more in things that were important to us. Alissa was able to dive into her work with Safe and Sound, where she was a much sought-after presenter and advocate for parents, children, schools, and legislatures wherever she went. She also found time to write a book, *An Unseen Angel*, describing her spiritual journey through grief and how she found ways to remain feeling close to Emilie.

From time to time, I also was invited to speak at small events and found the experiences very rewarding. At work, I was able to connect with families struggling in the NICU with deeper compassion and understanding. Mostly, though, as I had learned earlier, I continued to work on healing from all of my parts that needed healing, specifically starting with my childhood sexual abuse.

One day in 2015, after we had settled fully in, I was doing some mindfulness work at home, when I realized that, growing up, my family rarely spoke about what all of my siblings and I had endured at the hands of our abusers. The previous night Alissa had read a bedtime story to the girls containing a princess, a family member that died and in the end lived happily ever after. After hearing the story, Samantha pulled the fingers she had been sucking out of her mouth and proclaimed, "Hey, that's just like us!"

"What do you mean that's just like us?" Alissa asked in return.

"Well, they had someone in their family die, just like Emilie died in our family, and we are happy, too, just like them."

Samantha's comment touched me deeply and I was grateful it appeared easy for her to talk about what she was feeling. The more I thought about her comment, the more I realized that was not how my family growing up handled tough emotional topics. With what we had been through, there was a strong sense of the *we don't talk about that* mentality. And we didn't.

I wanted to understand better what had happened to me and my siblings so I could appreciate how those events affected me as an adult. I called my mother and asked her some questions. Then I called her again soon after. Over the course of a few months, we had many conversations because she finally felt able to speak candidly with me and answer hard questions. This level of vulnerability was rarely experienced among members of my family, and I felt it was the beginning of a healing process between me and my mother on a level I didn't realize was needed.

Once the healing between me and my mom was happening, I turned my attention to my siblings. It felt urgently important to hear *their* stories and comprehend what they had been through. I talked with them over the phone and in person when I was able to over the course of about six months. Being able to face my own abuse finally, I found I deeply cared how they had each been affected from their abuse, in their own way. I was humbled and grateful for their courage in sharing. It was amazing to me that after losing Emilie and opening up my heart to grief, I was being led to other areas in my life that sorely needed healing as well.

And I needed more. I began to see how the abuse had taken my voice and created an inability to own my emotional expression, especially regarding conflict. It left me, in certain situations, feeling impotent and weak when chaos and conflict were present. Recognizing these patterns, I launched a personal quest to learn as much as possible regarding my abuser and accompanying circumstances.

In therapy, I began to see how my present personal struggles and failings throughout life were connected to these traumas. So many decisions and actions brought great suffering for me that also extended to my wife and children when I was emotionally cut off, unavailable, or unresponsive. I learned that my "out-fun, out-wit, and out-run" defenses as a child contained many unhealthy coping mechanisms. Not wanting to be rejected or hurt by people I cared about, I used to lie a lot to stay out of trouble. Whether I had done anything wrong or not. I sought out forms of comfort that did not align with my moral or religious upbringing, which I constantly hid and felt tremendous shame for. This led to more lying and shame, which made me seek more comfort, and that cycle played out over and over as a child, a young adult, and now as a husband and father. The mental and emotional block I'd been feeling in my grief for Emilie began to make sense. A path opened for me to pursue further truth and healing.

By 2016, after speaking with almost everyone I could imagine, I realized that the information I had collected was mainly one-sided from the perspective of my own family. There were still gaps in the timeline and circumstances from my early childhood that I could not completely fill in. One evening, I realized that there were other sources I could try to contact . . . but was it worth the risk?

I remembered how, before our abuse came to light, my family and my abuser's family had been very good friends. We had vacationed together and spent a lot of time at each other's houses. Before everything blew up, I was really good friends with their youngest son. *Maybe he will be willing to talk with me?* Perhaps he could provide another, helpful perspective toward my healing. After all, we had been good friends, and what happened between our families wasn't either of our faults.

As I pondered following through with my idea, I realized that both of our fathers were capable of abusing children, and I grew concerned with my old friend's well-being. I wondered if he, too, had been victimized by either of them.

After tracking down his email and discussing my plan with Alissa and Deb, I drafted an email where I quickly explained my reasons for reaching out and asked if he would be willing to talk about a painful past.

The next afternoon, I received a reply. My heart jumped for a moment. Then I realized the response was not from my old friend, but from his father, Douglas Stoddard, the man responsible for the sexual abuse wrought upon me and my brothers. All I knew about Doug was that, thanks to a plea deal, he had only faced legal ramifications for the abuse he inflicted on my oldest brother. He did not serve any prison time, although he was placed on probation and forced to register as a sex offender for life. He never apologized or took any responsibility for any of his actions publicly or privately. In fact, he even failed to fulfill a court-ordered, face-to-face meeting with my brother after Stoddard falsely accused him of tape-recording their meeting and stormed out.

When I first recognized who the email was from, I was repulsed by the idea of even reading it. Very quickly, though, I felt something very old, yet very young calling out deep inside of me. I could choose to ignore feelings and shove them down again, *but where had that gotten me*? Instead, I sat with this feeling until it became clear this was the traumatized part I had been working for—the same part that blocked my grief work years before. This part was begging to be seen and heard; this part of me wanted me to read the email, fighting against my ancient coping strategies that always wanted to stay quiet, remain unseen, and never engage. I could no longer protect that part of me, but I could honor it.

In pursuit of healing and respect for this wounded child, I read the email, which contained an offer to speak with him directly, not his son.

Hell no!

But my wounded part was too fired up, too tired of hiding. Something came over me and I simply had to set up a meeting.

After consulting with Alissa and my therapist again, I felt as though this was something I had to do and was true to my healing process. This was about my childhood abuse, but it was also about the grief and the abuse I'd endured since December 14, 2012. I had willingly silenced a piece of myself, but now—surprising even me—I was ready to speak. I emailed him back, setting boundaries for our conversation. This, I said, was strictly about my healing process. I expected him to tell the truth. This was not about holding grudges—only responsibility and honesty.

We set up the meeting, and a few days later, I sat at my kitchen table and hit RECORD on my cell phone. I called the man responsible for so much pain and suffering in my family, and inside of me. His surprisingly high, effeminate voice greeted me. Then he began the conversation by telling me, "I hope you understand how hard this is for me?"

Are you freaking kidding me? Hard for you! I thought, while keeping my composure. "You are the one that requested to talk," I reminded him. "You don't have to if you don't want to." After a moment of silence on the other line, he finally started talking while I asked probing questions.

At one point, Stoddard blamed my father for *my* abuse. I gripped my cell phone, hard.

"Believe me, I know my dad is capable of horrible things, so if he had abused me, I would say so. But *you* are the one who snuck into your son's room when I slept over at your house. *You* are the one who laid down and sexually assaulted me."

During the conversation, every time he lied, he was met with a conflicting truth that I knew and I spoke aloud. After each fact was presented, he pivoted to another angle or tactic. I listened, rather fascinated, as he then tried to convince me that my little brother, James, "was so young he couldn't have remembered any abuse, so your parents made up a vicious lie to attack me!"

"Actually," I responded as calmly as possible—while almost exploding inside—"James was the first person to tell my parents what happened. James, without provocation, told my mom what you were doing to him. *Nobody* told him anything. He is the reason you got *caught* for what you did."

For over an hour, I encountered every form of manipulation, lies, and gaslighting imaginable. It was eerily similar to the tactics Jones used on air (and later in the courtroom) to avoid responsibility. It was infuriating. Still, each time, I simply stood up and spoke the truth for that wounded child who needed his story to be heard. This is what allowed his healing process to begin. I owned my voice, despite the other party's every effort to deflect accountability. I defended myself, my brothers, and—the truth.

After that phone call, I started to feel a monumental shift in how I approached my fears and insecurities. So many times, I'd allowed my fears to keep me from putting myself out there. Alissa and I said no to opportunities we were actually interested in or cared about, like the Remington lawsuit. I balked at opportunities for advocacy work through my employer about legislation for child health and safety because I didn't want to draw attention to myself. However, that experience helped me see that despite perceived risks, there could be great rewards if I just leaned into my fears more.

Later that year, Alissa and I were invited to participate in a fundraising gala for a wonderful non-profit organization called Art with Heart, which our non-profit, the Emilie Parker Art Connection, strongly supported. Art with Heart provides an amazing curriculum and activities to connect grieving children with the power of art therapy. Madeline and Samantha gobbled up their material enthusiastically in a way Alissa and I found to be helpful.

Previously, the idea of something like this would have left me feeling overly anxious, but we were making progress in both grief and healing, and this was for a wonderful cause. I found that after my phone call with Stoddard, I was more vocal in certain areas of my life. I could look new people in the eye when I met them. I was more comfortable and relaxed in public. And the fervor of Sandy Hook hoaxers felt more like a simmer instead of a roiling boil. We were excited to celebrate Emilie's legacy and the progress we had made as a family at the Art with Heart gala. Besides, we were able to spend a weekend in Seattle and stay at a nice hotel with the girls. So, we accepted.

The day before the event, our family drove up to Seattle and I dropped Alissa and the girls off in front of the hotel to check in, then left to park the car up the street. On my way back, Alissa sent me a text with the room number and said that Samantha had left her goggles in the van and they wanted to go swimming right away. After backtracking to retrieve the goggles, I was almost back to the hotel when a man on the sidewalk made eye contact with me—and wouldn't look away. He was easily over six feet tall, with dark hair and dressed like any other Seattle professional walking downtown after work.

His eyes were inquisitive. "Hey," he said, stopping me, "didn't you have a child that was killed?"

I hadn't been randomly recognized in a long time. "Yes, my daughter Emilie was killed at Sandy Hook Elementary," I said and reflexively offered my hand. I expected he would give some sort of condolences, as I had received hundreds of times before.

He looked at my hand, then stared at me for a few seconds. Suddenly I watched his face contort while his eyes darkened. He pursed his lips tight before spitting, "How the fuck do you sleep at night, you fucking son of a bitch?" His words were pure hatred and I stood still, shocked, as if I had just been bitten by a snake. He stepped directly in front of me and continued, "How much money did they give you? Huh? How much fucking money did they give you, you lying sack of shit?"

I froze and felt my blood boil while my hands and jaw clenched tight. Behind him, just across the street, was the hotel where my wife and daughters waited for me and the goggles inside my pocket. I needed to keep this man away from them—at all costs. Without saying a word, I turned around and started walking up the street away from the hotel.

The man didn't follow behind me, but rather kept pace on my side, continuing to spit his venom in my ear, his voice raised, yelling obscenities. I grew hot, and my entire face flushed as I became overcome with emotion in a way I had never experienced before. Everyone else on the crowded street seemed to disappear and the ancillary noise of the city faded away. I had never directly experienced so much vile hatred before in person. I felt myself start to panic.

I picked up my pace and so did he. "Huh, motherfucker? We all know no one was killed at Sandy Hook. The FBI fucked up and reported no one died. Emilie isn't real." The moment he said Emilie's name, I stopped walking and my whole body turned to face him.

"What did you say?" I said, feeling the anger explode like a volcano. "What did you say?" I yelled again.

We both stepped closer to each other, but before he uttered another sound, I began screaming.

"Don't you *ever* fucking say her name again!" We both stood for a second, staring, seething with rage for each other before we started yelling again.

"Who do you think you are? What the fuck have I ever done to you? What the fuck have I ever done to anyone?"

"Admit it, you're just a piece of shit actor and a liar!"

"My daughter was murdered in her school and you attack me? Fuck you!"

"Just tell me the truth. God is watching you and you're going to burn in hell."

"I don't owe you shit, you moronic dumbass . . . you don't *know* anything besides the garbage you listen to. Get the fuck away from me!"

I noticed the pedestrians on the crowded street had parted like the Red Sea around us, which broke my concentration briefly. I looked back at him just long enough to pity the world of lies and hatred he lived in. I wanted no part of it anymore.

I turned and walked up to another intersection with him in hot pursuit, continuing his tirade. When I reached the corner and turned right, he stopped and yelled one more profanity before he crossed the street in a different direction.

Completely overcome with rage, I could feel my heartbeat pounding in my ears. For the first time ever, I'd engaged with a conspiracist and felt the disgust emanating off of him, for who he thought I was. Purposely I walked around the block two more times, making sure he was nowhere to be found. Scanning in every direction, finally I headed back toward the hotel. I took deep breaths as I walked, trying to calm myself.

I had no idea how long I had been gone. Finally, when I felt like I had composed myself and that it was safe for my girls, for my family, I went up to the room.

Without a key, I knocked on the door and heaved another deep breath before Alissa opened it. Without a word between us, she took one look at me. "What happened to you?" she asked with both alarm and compassion in her eyes.

I stared back, bit my lip, and shook my head. She pulled me into the room, shut the door, cradled my face in her hands, and with deep concern, asked again, "Robbie, what happened to you?"

Chapter 8

What Is Wrong with Me?

"Please tell me—what happened? Robbie . . . Robbie?" Alissa pleaded, while I frantically paced back and forth in the small dark hallway of the hotel room until Alissa pulled me into the bathroom for some privacy.

I couldn't speak and kept shaking my head. Despite my unexpected outburst, every emotion not spilled on the street bubbled up inside of me, threatening to erupt. Years of pent-up sensations were stampeding toward an opening, having finally been given a fault line to escape. But I didn't know how to let them all free and my whole body fought to keep them constrained. After all, my two sweet young girls were just outside the hotel room's bathroom door.

My logical mind knew just how much my wife cared for me, and I could only imagine how worried she was at my sudden, distraught behavior. I couldn't get a handle on it, this wild fear of threat and this feverish, protective chaos in my mind and body. I could feel two distinct parts of myself battling for control. The part that wanted to finally let everything—not just what I was caught up in now but *everything*—out and the part that wanted to push it down even further, like I always had. Afraid of what could happen if I actually opened up.

Finally, I pulled her close. I took a breath, and then another. She waited patiently while I calmed myself enough to speak. Quietly, I began to utter a few words, and then it came out as a torrent, describing what transpired with the man on the street. My back was turned to the door, still anxious not to alert Madeline and Samantha that something might be wrong.

I constantly interrupted my own narrative with tears when I lost my composure, while reiterating, "I'm so glad you and the girls weren't there," over and over again.

Seeing that Alissa and the girls were spared from what I experienced solidified that I would continue to do everything—sacrifice anything—to carry this burden myself and keep them safe.

Reiterating the story with Alissa, feeling and seeing the shock, disgust, and burning rage in both that man and myself a second time made it so I couldn't deflect or reframe this experience as anything less than what it really was. It touched every one of my senses. I could feel, see, and hear the hatred pass between us. The smell of his cologne and taste of the exhaust from passing cars still lingered. We were making so much progress after our move. We were healing and opening up and felt safe. And I was livid how this man showed me that despite those successes the threats were never dormant. That healing from these wounds would always entail being subjected to people like Jones and his cronies.

Alissa listened intently as I paced the small bathroom, while I continued to release the energy and emotions still chomping to be expressed. Everything gushed toward the opening this experience created. If allowed, I could have stayed there for days, letting out not just the heat of the moment but everything I had repressed until then. Ultimately, though, only so much was able to make it through the fault line before my body sealed it back up. And Madeline and Samantha only had so much patience. They knocked on the door. "Can we go swimming now?" they asked with eager excitement oozing from their dulcet, unaware voices.

"Are you okay to go?" Alissa asked me tenderly. "I can take them and give you some time to settle down."

"No, I want to go; I need all of you right now," I responded, pulling the goggles out of my pocket. I took another deep breath, opened the door, and was greeted with excited cheers and jumps from the girls.

Before leaving, the ever astute and benevolent Madeline asked Alissa, "Is Dad okay?" We made it a goal to always be honest with our girls, in an age-appropriate manner, concerning anything to do with grief and conspiracy theorists. It was important that they heard this kind of information from us first and not from another source that could be confusing and hurtful to them. Like I was the morning after the press conference. I can't remember exactly when we first tried to explain to them that there were people who didn't believe that Emilie died and that we were all faking the Sandy Hook shooting. I do remember it feeling like I was showing them a picture of a giraffe and trying to convince them it was a horse. Over the years they would occasionally ask questions or pick up on things as kids do when parents aren't aware their kids are listening. They were aware that people like Alex Jones and Wolfgang Halbig existed and there were some bad things said about our family on the internet. So when Madeline asked if I was okay, we were able to explain that a man recognized me and was one of the people that thought Emilie didn't die. We told them he said some mean things about me and Emilie and I was pretty upset by what happened. We reassured them they were safe and they accepted the explanation, as just one of those things our family has to deal with. But the mere fact that my now eight- and seven-year-old daughters accepted that a stranger accosting me on the street was typical or even expected in our family was extremely troubling.

In between splashing pool games, Alissa and I continued processing what happened. It felt like all of the progress I had made individually, and we had made as a family, was washed away. Intense pangs of guilt and shame that I was the reason my family was in this dangerous situation coursed through me again. Then, I realized how my very presence might jeopardize Art with Heart's gala the next day. I couldn't bear the thought of that, so I thought it would be best if I skipped the event entirely. It broke my heart to think of missing out on something that would celebrate and cherish Emilie's legacy, but it terrified me to think that I might ruin the fundraiser by tempting a hoaxer to crash it. So I reached out to the charity's leadership and, with heavy embarrassment, told them what had happened and my concerns.

The Art with Heart group immediately rallied around us. Despite expressing their shock and disbelief at what transpired, they had no concerns about me continuing to participate. I accepted their reassurances but insisted we meet with the hotel's management and security teams after dinner, just in case.

The following day, the hotel management introduced me to their head of security, who had made arrangements to ensure the event went off without a hitch. This helped me relax and be able to appreciate the reason we came here in the first place. During the program portion of the gala, Madeline and Samantha were a huge hit. It was so fun to watch them perform their parts so well. Alissa and I spoke about our family's experiences with this wonderful organization and the amazing healing power of art therapy they provided for our daughters.

We had a lovely experience. Like any moment where people come together in Emilie's spirit of love, kindness, and playful creativity, I felt her presence beside me. The rest of our time in Seattle with

Art with Heart was wonderful and productive, helping them raise tens of thousands of dollars for their cause. It felt great that despite everything that happened, we followed through and achieved what we had set out to do. However, there were signs that my encounter with the man on the street had brought a change . . . in me.

On the elevator with Madeline on the way down to the lobby, the doors opened, and we stopped as another guest entered. I looked up to see a man staring at us, which unnerved me. Immediately, I pulled Madeline behind me to put myself between her and this stranger. But the man simply entered the elevator, smiled, turned around, and waited for the doors to close—just like any other ordinary person.

My reaction surprised me. Though I had been fueled by a desire to protect since Emilie's death, I had never become so viscerally defensive and responded so firmly in that way. I worried that I might have frightened Madeline. Yet, at that moment, it also felt necessary and exactly what I should have done. After all, the man on the street seemed totally normal but left no doubt about his thoughts and feelings about who he thought I was. How was I supposed to know if the man on the elevator was similar? But we lived our lives constantly aware that there are millions of people that feel the same way. Living with that constant tension is draining, knowing there are people around you with the same feelings and never knowing who would stay quiet and who would feel motivated to do something.

A thought kept circling in my head. How many videos and pieces of conspiracy material had that man ingested in order to recognize me on a random street, four years and three thousand miles removed from Sandy Hook?

It was a disturbing question to contemplate. Other thoughts and questions grew stronger and repeated in my mind in the years to come. How many out there are just like him? Who else, at work, church, or anywhere around me feels the same way and says nothing? Who might actually do something?

These perpetual thoughts completely changed how I viewed and engaged with the world. The momentum I had garnered in my personal progress through grief work and facing my traumas lost all steam after our trip to Seattle. I finally used my voice against my childhood abuser and felt able to expand my comfort zone and what did it get me? I was immediately attacked and put my family in danger. Without even realizing it, I fell back into my childhood protective stance, where it was safer to stay quiet, remain unseen, and not engage. It was better to keep trying to out-fun, out-wit, and out-run these traumatic events. And I ran.

In almost every interaction outside of my home or work, I became even more withdrawn than before. I felt I was a burden, exposing everyone around me to this dark and poisonous side of the world. My body resorted back to old habits: keeping my head down, eyes peeled and remaining as invisible as possible. No matter how much time or distance we were away from Sandy Hook, it still wasn't safe to venture out into the meadow.

Down in Austin, Texas, Jones continued to produce and publish Sandy Hook–related content five years after the shooting. For years he had been advised against continuing his claims and attacks on Sandy Hook families from within his inner circle. These messages of warning and potential liability appeared to have found some traction when Jones aired what he titled his "Final Statement on Sandy Hook" in November 2016, just a few weeks after I was accosted in Seattle.

This twenty-minute segment began with him sitting behind his huge news desk with papers everywhere, saying, "This message is not for the fake news media. But I do want to reach out to the victims . . . reach out to my listeners as well and just clarify where I stand on the reported tragedy at Sandy Hook. All I know is that the official story about Sandy Hook has more holes in it than Swiss cheese."

The next seventeen minutes were spent reminding his audience about specific conspiracies or talking points that had already been explained or debunked. He highlighted the reporting of a second shooter, ridiculed President Obama's press conference where he cried talking about the murdered children, falsely claimed that Anderson Cooper was using a green screen, said that the Sandy Hook school had been closed for years before the shooting, and again showed my press conference clip while calling me disgusting. "Then we see footage of one of the reported fathers of the victims, Robbie Parker, doing classic actor training, where he's laughing and joking and then they say, 'Hey, we are live,' and he goes, 'Oh.'" Then he began a melodramatic reenactment of my deep breathing and crying.

Finally, he tried to end the statement with, "Why should anybody fear an investigation if they have nothing to hide? There are other mass shootings that are very suspicious . . . but, this particular case, they are so scared of an investigation. So you got what you want. I'm going to start reinvestigating Sandy Hook and everything else that happened with it. I'm Alex Jones signing off . . . but ask yourself, what is so strange about Sandy Hook and that tragedy?"

Jones's tone transformed at this point from being inquisitive to one that feigned sympathy.

"But I will say this, finally, that my heart goes out to all parents that lose children. Whether it's stabbings or car wrecks or stranglings or blunt force trauma or murder . . . whatever the case is, I'm a parent and my heart goes out to all parents that have lost children in these tragic events. And so, if children were lost in Sandy Hook, my heart goes out to each and every one of those parents, and the people that say they are parents, that I see on the news." Here his emotional-sympathy well became totally dry, his posture stiffened, and his face constricted as his voice turned menacing.

"The only problem is, I've watched a lot of soap operas and I've seen actors before," he said, his eyes widening and voice growling, "and I know when I'm watching a movie and when I'm watching something real." He then sat up and leaned forward in an offensive posture before pointing at the camera. "Let's look into Sandy Hook."

Instead of this being his final statement on Sandy Hook, throwing a little empathy and moving on, he doubled down. It seemed he tried to stop, but in real time he diverted on air and just couldn't do it. This promise to reinvestigate and subsequent call to action rejuvenated his audience. Jones was again rewarded. I would find out later that over $103,000 flowed into *Infowars* on that day alone, and $165 million between 2015 and 2018.

It was impossible for us to move forward with our lives, to feel safe, because just as we were getting comfortable, Jones would stoke the flames again. It was as if he knew when his grip was loosening on us, and try as he might, he couldn't let us go.

About seven months later, in June of 2017, it appeared that perhaps Jones's heart may have grown a size bigger when he showed a special Father's Day tribute video to parents from Sandy Hook. Appearing tranquil, staring up and away at some ethereal presence off camera, Jones talked about holding his infant daughter that morning, and how his heart broke for parents who have lost children. In the video he offered "sincere condolences" to the parents of the slain children in Newtown, Connecticut, before offering an invitation to "contact me and open up a dialogue" for more "unity and peace in our country."

In reality, the video was nothing more than part of a two-hour, self-serving, counterprogramming special to neutralize his infamous interview with Megyn Kelly, the then current NBC and former Fox News anchor, set to air the same night. Jones worked hard to keep the interview from airing and complained publicly that NBC and Megyn Kelly lied to him, set him up, and doctored footage to make him look bad. When I heard his complaints, the irony of him moaning about doctored footage to make him look bad while people lied was not lost on me.

Jones wasn't the only one who didn't want that interview to air. Many of the Sandy Hook families pleaded with NBC not to give him a national platform to spread his lies to a broader audience. One mother, Nelba Márquez-Green, whose daughter Ana Grace was murdered in the same room as Emilie, gave interviews with national media outlets to voice her objections to the piece with Jones. Megyn Kelly had previously been selected to host a gala event by one prominent Sandy Hook–related charity, who then felt obligated to rescind the invitation over the Jones interview. NBC rejected all of these complaints and aired the controversial interview on Father's Day, 2017. As the families suspected, the interview did little to hold Jones accountable, but it did reignite the fire of his fan base.

For weeks after the interview aired, there was an uptick in conspiracy traffic trying to defend Jones by resuscitating brain-dead lies, with another round of YouTube videos, emails to the Art Connection, and direct messages attacking family members on social media. The bitter cherry on top of this squall of harassment was the handwritten letter sent directly to our home.

Postmarked from Portland, Oregon, with no return address, the letter simply stated:

> Dear Robbie,
> I sent the sheriff out to see you a few weeks ago.
> I'm surprised your not in prison yet.
> There are going to be a few people going to prison.
> KP

The content in the letter appeared quite timid compared to other messages being lobbed in our direction. However, this letter was a direct hit on any sense of anonymity we may have had. KP, or Kevin Purfield, was the same man who made our friend Brooke want to vomit on the phone and penned the letter we gave to the FBI, and the same man who had been arrested back in 2013 when we lived on the other side of the country.

His arrest led to a plea deal involving prison time and parole, which seemed to do very little in rehabilitating this unwell individual. Within weeks after his release from custody, he made the effort to find me and again write a letter to my new home. But this time, there was no longer thousands of miles separating us, as he now lived only thirty minutes from my front door. The letter was felt as a warning for both Alissa and myself with an implied message of *I know where you are and how to find you.*

Once again, our home did not feel safe or secure and was no longer just *ours* after we'd worked incredibly hard to make it so. We had purposefully bought property in a more rural area that we felt meshed with our healing. We worked in the garden, picked blueberries, and ate dinners outside in a gazebo shaded by large maple trees. The girls chased their chickens and caught frogs in the nearby pond. Now we were back to paying attention to every car that drove down the dusty dirt road inside our spread-out neighborhood. The space we sought for healing now felt like an impediment to our safety.

Alissa and the girls felt like they were left unprotected in an isolated area when I was at work overnight. After an incident at school, Samantha, who is a very compassionate and sensitive person, began a ritual every night, methodically going around the house and checking doors and windows making sure that they were secure. She had heard a boy make an offhand comment to someone else in their third-grade class: "Be careful or else I could get my dad's gun and do a school shooting."

Samantha quipped back at him to quit talking like that. "It's not funny," she bravely told him. "My sister died in a school shooting."

"That's not true."

"Yes, it is. My sister died at Sandy Hook."

"Then you're a liar," he sniggered back, "and your whole family are liars."

Within days we installed a home security system, complete with internal and external cameras. Alissa, through her school safety work, contacted a colleague with expertise in security and threat assessment. Fortunately, this person had personal contacts with the Portland Police Department and helped them understand our specific situation and concerns.

We met with the girls' school administrators, giving them pictures of Purfield and warned them about potentially receiving phone calls, emails, or visits from him. I did the same with the hospital security team in case he called or showed up looking for me.

Within a few months, we learned from Alissa's colleague that the Portland Police performed a surprise visit and search of Purfield's residence, where they removed weapons that violated court orders and the terms of his parole.

The relentless threat from new conspiracy material being produced while living with the knowledge that anyone, anywhere, at any time could risk my family's safety was mentally and emotionally draining. Feeling like there were no more places to run, my only option appeared to be to withdraw even deeper internally.

The mental and emotional toll was compounded by the fact that externally I made myself appear as though everything was fine when I had to engage with family, friends, and colleagues. To the best I could manage, people around me received the message that neither grief nor conspiracists defined me, nor had any power over my life. I didn't want my girls to see or feel the fear that roiled inside of me, and I did whatever I could to shield them from it.

I naturally defaulted back into old and unhealthy coping mechanisms where I lied to everyone, especially myself, about how this was affecting me. Creating the cycle of shame, lies, coping all over. Again, Alissa noticed and felt these changes and approached me with her concerns. Which I promptly dismissed because I was too scared to admit to the reality of what she was witnessing. This time, though, this cycle felt more intense and the shame, lies, coping, and especially my actions, followed suit.

As I lied and repressed my emotions, my ability to control my anger worsened. Most of the time it was not on display, but I knew it was there. Other times it was noticeable and felt by everyone around me but ignored after attempts to help me see it were rebuffed. Every once in a while, though, it came out with the potential for damage and unintended consequences.

For months I noticed that the hose spigot outside my front door had been leaking. When a fresh layer of algae became visible on the corner of our porch, I could no longer ignore it. As any responsible homeowner in my situation, I looked up videos on how to fix a leaky spigot and went straight to Home Depot and bought a two-dollar part to fix the problem. I took the spigot apart only to realize the part I had bought didn't work and I needed more parts. After more videos and another fifteen dollars at Home Depot, I replaced the valve and stem only to have it leak even worse than before I started. Fed up with videos, I returned to Home Depot for the third time and spoke with a worker, then walked out with a completely new hose bib for thirty dollars.

By this point I was beyond annoyed. So when the new hose bib would not thread properly onto the pipe inside the wall, I could feel my anger simmering toward a boil. As my fifteen-minute, two-dollar project entered into its third hour, third trip to Home Depot, and inched toward fifty dollars, Samantha approached me. She needed my help with something that she had been waiting to ask me all afternoon. My previous reply of, "I'll be there in a few minutes when I'm done with this," to her initial request was long overdue. Seeing all the wrenches, screwdrivers, drill, and now a chisel with dismantled pipe parts and water everywhere, she approached with trepidation.

"Dad . . . when do you think you can help me with—" she began.

I started my interruption with, "Does it look like I'm done here, Samantha!" I was trying to control my voice. I wasn't yelling but my sharp tone and frustration from the project began spilling out.

"You see this pipe?" I asked, holding the pipe. "I can't get it to do what I want . . ." and bashed it against the cement porch.

She flinched at the loud *bang* and I could visibly see her squirm, uncomfortable by my behavior. Big tears formed in her eyes but didn't drop, like my heart did in my chest watching her reaction. I tried my best to console her, explaining that I was upset because of the project, not at her. I reassured her she had done nothing wrong. She nodded in agreement and accepted my apology with a quivering voice. "It's okay."

It wasn't okay. It felt like she agreed with my explanation with more hope than belief. Seeing the caution in her approach showed me I was radiating more negativity than I realized, and she was absorbing it. I knew I was out of balance with my anger and had been for a long time. I knew I was feeling the effects from it and was trying hard to address the issue myself. For the first time I really saw the negative impact it had on those around me. Trying to deal with the issue myself didn't protect them from the problem—it exposed them to it.

At that moment I felt defeated. The plumbing project showed me how well I could handle problems on my own. How what I thought would be an easy fix by myself could unravel into a longer project with a bigger price.

All of this was compounded by the increasing wave of mass shootings that continued to take place across the country—with seemingly no end in sight. Some shootings, like the ones in Roseburg, Oregon, and Marysville, Washington, were too close to home. Between 2013 and 2018, there were 34 shootings in schools alone, killing 60 while injuring 119 people.

The news after every shooting initiated what became a familiar cycle. Alissa and I discovered that there was a unique pain, knowing that other families are experiencing a loss that only certain people can fully comprehend. Tributes were paid to each victim and makeshift memorials would spring up and be used as B-roll for media footage. In our desensitized society, with each shooting, the time for reflection and public mourning shrank.

Since Sandy Hook, it appeared that every time gunshots rang out in public places, everyone from politicians to media to your crazy uncle on Facebook didn't take cover, but rather grabbed their soapboxes, sprinted to their respective corners of society, took a defensive position, and prepared to attack. Guns—not victims, not survivors—quickly became the focus of everyone's attention. Pundits debated, op-eds were written, social media went berserk, and conspiracies continued to flourish in these now well-fertilized soils.

Thoughts and prayers were verbally expressed, but I had come to doubt that they were truly offered sincerely by all who repeated the phrase as part of a press release or public statement. Those that offered thoughts and prayers, but no real action, seemed content to accept that it was either God's fault or God's will that these tragedies continued unimpeded, instead of *using* the tools or talents God may have given us to find the remedies on our own.

One morning I walked into work at the hospital dreading the day ahead. The previous day, reports of another school shooting (sadly there have been too many to remember which one) made headlines across the country. This was challenging. As I waded through the emotional toll I felt after every such event, while balancing my work responsibilities, my colleagues in the NICU were also keenly aware of my presence. Like I always did, I tried to put on my best *I'm fine* face. But on days like this, their compassion would focus on how I was processing the recent news. I sincerely appreciated their concern but constantly reassuring everyone I was okay when I wasn't was exhausting. I could never fully express what I really felt, concerned that it might overwhelm them and me while we cared for our vulnerable babies.

Another odd phenomenon I discovered that occurred after a shooting happened was how some people, while checking in with me, felt the need to share their opinions about guns. One wonderful nurse entered my office that morning expressing her heartfelt condolences before exclaiming, "I can't believe those guns are still allowed! It's sickening that politicians are too chickenshit to stand up and do something."

Five minutes later, another, equally fantastic nurse came into my office, gave me a hug, and with tears expressed how sorry she was "for what you've been through. I was sick when I heard the news," she cried, "and immediately thought how hard these shootings must be for you. And it just pisses me off that every time this happens, people want to make it all about guns. When guns have nothing to do with it! These people are mentally ill and need help and it drives me crazy that nobody cares enough to do anything about it." Then she stormed out.

These back-to-back experiences left me bewildered. I had never uttered to anyone, ever, what my complex opinions and feelings were regarding gun rights and gun control. Both nurses, whom I respected and admired, in their zeal to defend a position that was inspired and fueled by tribalism, friendship, algorithms, and echo chambers, automatically assumed that I agreed with them. For me, it wasn't about either of these things. Yes, I'd formed my own opinions over the years, but my broken, beating heart still thought of Emilie. I thought of the families who were now suffering an unimaginable loss. I did not want to be a spokesperson. I wanted to be a father.

By that evening, toward the start of the night shift, I had spent an entire day holding my true emotions in check so I could outwardly show everyone how well I was holding it all together. I was exhausted and in the mood for a break when Monica stormed into the NICU late for her night shift.

Monica is a tall, strong, wickedly smart nurse and never late for work. Her usual soft and welcoming brown eyes were fiery as she passed me to get her charge nurse report, offering a curt, "Sorry I'm late," to her counterpart. Everything about this scenario was completely off from the usual fun and charismatic Monica we were used to. Now it was my turn to be concerned and worried if she was all right.

A short while later, Monica approached me in the hallway with much of the same upset energy she had exhibited when she first entered the NICU. "I need to talk to you," she insisted before entering a vacant patient room for some privacy. The barren room, with its empty incubator and blank monitors, quickly filled with an intense emotion that made it feel alive. Confused and concerned, I looked at Monica while she paced, before she stopped and blurted out, "How do you do it, Robbie? I don't get how you can stand it."

I watched her wipe hot tears from her eyes as she continued, "I just can't believe the things people say about you." Then she started telling me how her aunt posted and shared some Sandy Hook conspiracy propaganda on Facebook. Monica was appalled: she knew that conspiracies about my family existed, but this was the first time she actually experienced it for herself. As she described how disgusted and hurt she felt, I was struck by the magnitude of the loss. Lives had been lost, but our broader sense of trust, kindness, and compassion also seemed to be shattered after each of these events.

Her tears kept flowing as she recounted how she sent her aunt messages to take back what she said and delete them. After no response and watching her aunt actively commenting online with other people, she decided they needed to talk face-to-face.

Monica left her house early for work so she could stop at her aunt's house on the way. She tried speaking calmly with logic and reason, telling her aunt she knew someone whose daughter was killed at Sandy Hook. That these are real people and what she was saying and spreading was hurtful. Unfortunately, Monica learned for herself, as I had, that logic and reason in the conspiracy world actually entices an argument. The aunt fought back, screaming, calling her a liar and saying she couldn't know anyone whose child died because it *never happened.*

Monica's tears finally stopped and her voice softened. "I'm so sorry, Robbie. I can't believe one of my own family members could actually believe and say those things."

I didn't know what to say. I felt awful that she had experienced something that I'd grown accustomed to. I tried to console her. "I'm sorry you saw those things too—"

"How can you stand it, Robbie?" she interrupted, reiterating softly with a hoarse voice, her compassionate tears bubbling again. "How can you stand people disrespecting your daughter that way?"

Her question pierced me unexpectedly, but I did my best to reassure her that I try to focus on the good. I even gave her my spiel about "rising above the bad to show them they aren't winning." Though there was truth in that message, the words felt hollow and dishonest. It was hard right now for me to see the good—and I didn't feel like I was rising above anything.

After Monica walked away, her piercing question, "*How can you stand people disrespecting your daughter that way?*" left me feeling weak and uncomfortable from a harsh realization brought on from her experience. Why is Monica more upset than I am about this?

Why does she feel hurt, while I resort to silver linings and platitudes? I kept asking myself, "What is wrong with me?" I stayed up most of that night in deep reflection, exploring where my fiery desire to protect Emilie's name and memory had gone.

My childhood coping strategies were hurting me more than helping. Unfortunately, I was too deep in my hole to see it.

Chapter 9
Awakening

In February 2018, news broke out across the country about yet another mass shooting in an American school. Toward the end of Valentine's Day at Marjory Stoneman Douglas High School, in Parkland, Florida, seventeen people were killed and seventeen more were injured by a nineteen-year-old alumni of the school—simply because he wanted to.

As expected, the cycle began all over again. The shock, horror, and disbelief naturally rose, peaked, and subsided in the time frame of a regular news cycle. Frustratingly, one community official declared in an interview, "You know, there's no playbook for something as unimaginable as this, so we are doing the best we can."

That was not true.

In the years since Sandy Hook and other shootings, the playbook is redundantly clear for those willing to see it—playing out like an awful déjà vu for a growing number of families who are forced to live through them.

Once again, lines were quickly drawn, fingers were pointed, debates from national media channels to social media networks rolled on, and conspiracists jumped on their bandwagons quicker than ever. It was all with the same arguments, tactics, and motivations, just a new location and datapoints for everyone to argue over while the impacted families tried to make sense of their losses.

When the news broke, Alissa and I walked through our own playbook and checked in with each other to see if the other one had "heard the news yet." We waited and responded to kind people checking in to see if we were doing okay. When we saw the girls, we told them and made ourselves available to answer questions. We made it a point to proactively talk to the girls about these shootings as they occurred so they didn't hear about it from someone else that could be less sensitive to their actual needs. Then we distracted ourselves with life again, took the girls to activities, remembered to get dinner started on time, all in an effort to be a normal family. Because what else could we do?

What I didn't expect this time was a phone call from a church acquaintance who had moved away from the Pacific Northwest to Florida. After quick pleasantries he got straight to the point. "I assume you've heard about the shooting in Parkland, Florida?"

"Yes, I have . . . Wait, you didn't move there, did you?" I asked with concern, trying to remember how old his kids were. His family was fine, but he explained that another family in his congregation was not. Their teenage daughter was one of the victims.

"Would you and Alissa be willing to talk with them? You know, if they would want to and if you both felt comfortable with it?"

Of course we were okay with that but also confided that we don't claim to have some magic potion but are available to listen and help any way we could. After all this time, I can still find myself at a loss for what to say in the face of death and tragedy—just like everybody else. "Just one more thing before you go. Let them know there's no rush or expectation for them to do anything," I said. "It is an open-ended invitation that they are free to use whenever, however, and for as long as they'd like."

That last request seemed to have been delivered and received well, since we did not hear from that family for quite some time after the shooting. I honored that, because when I looked back at my own experience, it was clear to me how *sacred* the early grief process was. Those first moments and days were the closest I was going to be to Emilie ever again, when her smell still lingered in her room and her voice rang fresh in my ears—before it all turned into memories. Too many of my own, early grief experiences had been hijacked, so I didn't want to intrude on that time with this family.

About a month after the shooting in Parkland, I received another unexpected phone call, this time from a Sandy Hook father. I did not know this father very well as we hadn't had many opportunities to connect when we lived in Connecticut. Without much to get caught up on, small talk was easily bypassed and allowed him to dive right into why he called. "I wanted to let you know that myself and some other Sandy Hook folks have spoken with an attorney in Texas about going after Alex Jones for defamation."

I paused, and let that sink in. The idea of going directly after Alex Jones certainly piqued my interest, but I wasn't sure why he was calling to tell me about it. The notion of engaging with and provoking someone like Alex Jones had never crossed my mind.

"These lawyers are very sincere and are willing to take up the case," he continued. "There is something about suing Jones in Texas, in his own backyard, that I think will really send a message." Then he got to the point. "I know you have been a target of Jones and hoaxers for years . . . so . . . would you want to join the lawsuit with us?"

His question surprised me and, once again, I felt myself split in two. The first was a desire to engage and *do something* to combat this constant threat. The second was my long-standing coping strategies screaming at me to do nothing if I wanted to keep my family safe.

I managed to tell this father that I appreciated his call and consideration, but would need time to think it over, and we hung up. The moment I brought up the idea of joining a lawsuit to Alissa, she was equally apprehensive.

"I think it's great somebody wants to do it," she told me, "but I don't feel comfortable being *those* people."

"Besides," I said with a nod, "we've worked so hard to create a level of autonomy for ourselves and give the girls the chance to have their own lives."

"Exactly. We've worked extremely hard and it's getting better . . ."

We were silent for a moment.

"But they *still* come after me, so what can we do about that?" I asked, my voice distant, trying to give the warring sides of my emotions an outlet.

"They still come after you, which means they come after *us,*" Alissa said. "How do you think that will go if you join a lawsuit?" It was not a warning, but a sincere question. I was not the only one trying to decipher between our family's safety and the desire not to be held down by our fears any longer.

We played it out in conversation, considering the cost-benefit ratio to join the lawsuit. We not only analyzed the risk of jeopardizing the work we had put in over the years to create a sense of safety and anonymity, but I worried also about the stigma of being "sue happy," not to mention being judged for using Emilie's death to "get money."

In the end, the desire to stay quiet won out. We decided against joining the families suing Alex Jones in Texas—while truly wishing the best and success for those families that did. After the decision was made, I didn't reflect on it again. It felt like the right thing for our family to do. There was no secret desire that lingered and I never regretted it. And we continued to go about our lives.

Months later, the Parkland parents reached out. Ryan and Kelly Petty had lost their fourteen-year-old daughter, Alaina. In society we say "lost," because it feels like a more palatable term. However, losing something either happens by accident or because it was forgotten over time. In speaking with Ryan and Kelly, it was clear that Alaina wasn't lost. She certainly had not been forgotten and the shooting was no accident but an act of willful and deliberate murder. Her life was stolen, just as Emilie's had been. Period. Neither of them had been able to express their full potential, and the world suffered a loss because of it.

Kelly's soft voice, full of grief and a broken heart, asked, "Does the pain ever get easier to live with? Everyone says it will get better with time, but to me it seems like it is getting worse." Alissa and I looked at one another, squeezing each other's hands. Our eyes were wet, though they couldn't see. Ryan, we could tell, came to the phone call with an energy that spoke of his heated desire to do advocacy work—just like many parents before him whose children had been senselessly murdered at school.

Hearing their personal stories so close on the heels of the shooting felt like stepping back in time. The way they expressed their pain and their desires to find meaning in their daughter's death felt all too similar. Deep inside of me, I became aware of a vibrating sensation that started low in my chest, reverberating and quickening as it transmitted out toward my fingertips. I felt Emilie's absence like a tangible ache inside of me, even as I worked to stay present and listen with the Pettys. Suddenly, I heard something that triggered an even stronger reaction.

"What did you say?" I asked, really wanting to make sure I heard them correctly.

"I'm sorry, can you repeat that?"

"Ryan," Kelly repeated patiently, "did an interview for the media about Alaina, shortly after the shooting. Right afterward, we started being attacked and nasty, demeaning videos about Ryan showed up almost immediately online."

"My gosh! I'm so sorry; that is so horrific," Alissa chimed in before Kelly continued.

"Yes, it has just been so awful and so scary. I'm really glad that you guys didn't have to experience anything like that after your daughter was killed."

Alissa and I stared at each other, not knowing exactly what to say. We were here to listen and allow *them* to express themselves as much as possible. We didn't want to insert our experiences into theirs as if this was some sort of competition. It wasn't.

We listened to Ryan explain how he tried to get the videos taken down, but couldn't. They shared how violated they felt that people could actually produce and spread such ugly things about Ryan, Alaina, and their family. I forced myself to stay still and continued to listen, even while my blood began to boil, and I could feel my heart pounding so hard it felt like it was outside of my chest.

By the time the call ended, the vibrations in my chest erupted. I sprang from my seat, startling Alissa, her eyes wide. I was incensed beyond reason. "The same exact thing is happening to them—in the exact same way!" I yelled. "What's the point?" I screamed as I questioned the heavens, pacing and flailing my arms about wildly. "These people spread this crap, always at someone else's expense, and for what? Why!"

Alissa was watching me. No longer startled, she asked, "What is it exactly that is making you so upset?" As if daring me to let my anger loose. Aside from my experience in Seattle, Alissa had watched me hold my emotions back or rebuff her invitations for years. Either unwilling or unable to open up and share more deeply. After this call she saw the fault line open up again and wanted to keep it open before I closed it off.

"They are being robbed of their grief, Alissa!" I yelled again into the atmosphere, not at her. "We've been *exactly* where they have been; we know what is being stolen from them. They just need to grieve, they need to support their other kids, and they are being attacked. We know what it feels like *and they shouldn't be feeling it; they did nothing wrong*." I raised my fists up to the sky. "It's never going to end! Not for us, and not for the Pettys, either."

It was uncomfortable letting this much anger out at once. I tried to collect my wits and the version of Robbie that kept everything together. I was trembling with rage. This time, there was no battle over what I should do or how I should act. My fury was so strong I had no choice but to give in. I stopped pacing, and took deep breaths, but the fire was too hot. Every time I thought about the Pettys, it grew.

"What were we taught growing up? Ignore a bully, they will go away, right? But they aren't going away and it's not just us; it's not just Sandy Hook. It's them; it's all of us! Conspiracists are only getting bolder with their tactics. And for what? So those 'truthers' can play make-believe and pretend this isn't real? Screw them! Screw them for hurting people and getting themselves off playing their stupid games!"

I was over five years down the same road the Pettys were just starting. It didn't feel right, making them encounter the same things we had already endured. Suddenly, I no longer felt comfortable with the idea of doing nothing.

Shortly after our call with the Petty family, Alissa left for Florida, for a weekend retreat with some other Sandy Hook moms from our Healing Hearts group. After we moved away from Newtown, this was something they tried to do at least once a year together. I was grateful that there she would get to hang out with Michele Gay, Joey's mom, who was also Alissa's cofounder of Safe and Sound

Schools, as well as mutual friend, Tricia Pinto, among many others. These retreats were cathartic for Alissa and the other mothers. They got to be together, reminisce, and grieve in a way that only they knew how. Outside of our new group at the Dougy Center, Alissa didn't have other opportunities to be with people who could be supportive to her. Admittedly, being mostly shut down and not opening up made Alissa become more of a support for me than I was for her. I wasn't aware at the time, but some distance was building between the two of us on that front and I'm sure these retreats with other moms who could support and open up with her were refreshing.

I was cleaning up after an awesome mom's-out-of-town, dad-inspired take-out dinner when Alissa called out of the blue. Although I missed her terribly when she was gone, I loved getting special one-on-two time with Madeline and Samantha—something Alissa got way more of than I did. We stayed up late taking turns picking movies and making late runs to the store for more root beer float supplies. All while the dad jokes flowed like water. Thoughts of lawsuits or Alex Jones were far from my mind when I answered my phone.

"Hey, babe, what's up?"

Alissa's voice was fast and animated, as it gets when her mind is racing. "Robbie, I've been talking with Tricia about the lawsuits against Alex Jones."

"Oh, tell her hi for me," I said, oblivious to where this conversation was heading. "What does she have to say about it?"

"That she thinks you should join!"

Alissa, like a buzzing bee at a lilac bush, tried to catch me up to speed on everything she and Tricia talked about. Starting with another lawsuit that I didn't know about, which had been filed in Connecticut. How I had already spoken with the one father who asked us to join them in the case against Jones in Texas and why we decided not to. How Tricia and Dean had read the Connecticut lawsuit and felt like it had a lot of merit. Tricia, whose son Jack was killed, was a lawyer by training and met her husband, Dean, while they were in law school together, so their opinion intrigued me. She started to tell me why Tricia felt we should reconsider our decision to not join a lawsuit but got jumbled up on some details, then abruptly just said, "Here, I'll just have you talk to Tricia."

Tricia's voice, which felt so familiar and safe, melted any angst I was feeling like butter on a warm biscuit. "Alissa told me you guys talked with a family from Parkland," Tricia said, "and that the call really set you off."

"Yeah, that conversation opened up a lot of emotions for me," I admitted.

"That's so funny to me because I told Alissa, 'I can't picture Robbie ever getting upset.'"

As we talked, she explained that the lawsuit filed in Connecticut was really solid. She hadn't read the Texas case, but that Connecticut has a state unfair sales practice law that in its simplest terms means it is illegal to lie to consumers in order to sell a product.

The rest of our exchange centered around everything she found interesting about the lawsuit and where she felt like it was the strongest. I listened intently.

"Robbie," she said, "your name is all over that thing." A majority of the evidence they had against Alex Jones were things he had said about me on air, stating my full name with pictures and videos. She also said that because my name was mentioned so much I could easily be called to testify, perhaps even for both the plaintiffs and the defense. Meaning, even if I wanted to stay silent, I might be forced to tell my story anyway. And if Jones's defense team called me to testify, how I answered could be used against the Sandy Hook families. Tricia also told me that the law firm was the same firm that sued Remington Firearms on behalf of a group of Sandy Hook parents. At that point I didn't know what families had banded together to file the lawsuit or how it got to this point, but everything Tricia was telling me was intriguing. Like Alissa, my mind was racing.

"Look, it's up to you, there's no pressure," she said reassuringly, "but if there's anyone I know that should sue Alex Jones, it is you. Just think it over, okay?"

When Alissa took the phone back, we agreed to think about it on our own until she got home and we could talk it over together.

While the girls were asleep, I took the time to read over the entire lawsuit filed as *Lafferty et al. v. Alex Jones et al.* in detail. It was a bizarre experience to see so much of my life being repeated back at me in a legalese tone, where my real-life experiences seemed to be a source of fodder for some horrific, but nonfiction fairy tale. Seeing it all laid out, the weight of what we'd been through hit me hard. Everything was articulately laid out in factual terms almost devoid of emotion. There were no distractions; there was no passage of time from one point to the next. These weren't just isolated random experiences. So much of what Jones said and did over five years to that point was all there in black and white.

Just like after our call with the Pettys, my emotional levee broke and the internal battle resumed. I paced around the house, then outside back and forth through the gazebo. I wanted to engage, I wanted to join and fight. This was how I could do something. But that entailed going after the man that the Kevin Purfields, the man in Seattle, and tens of millions of other people deemed as their leader. My walls were down and I spent the next few days waiting for Alissa to come home, picking up the rubble. Each piece represented a valid emotion of either fear of the unknown, anger from the past, concern for the future, or a now-fiery desire to help.

When Alissa and I finally spoke after her arrival, all I could muster was that I was open, even considering the idea of joining the lawsuit. We both acknowledged that our reasons for not participating in the other lawsuit were still valid. They could not just be tossed aside by another wave of emotion. If we were to join, our reasons would have to be equally valid and true to our values.

We had work to do. First, we sent the complaint filed in Connecticut to some of the most preeminent First Amendment attorneys in the country—one even retained by a major news corporation—so we could obtain their thoughts and opinions. All of them, with their decades of experience, advised us in exactly the same way Tricia Pinto had. We heard multiple times from multiple parties that the complaint was solid, and also that I would most likely be called as a witness for both sides. "So, you might as well join the suit," one lawyer said. "Let your voice be heard for yourself and not for anybody else's agenda."

I then spoke with the firm that filed the lawsuit on behalf of the families in Connecticut. I explained my concerns and apprehensions as well as my feelings for and against joining the suit. Josh Koskoff and Matthew Blumenthal, who wrote the complaint, listened intently and validated both my concerns and desires. They also gently reassured me that the choice to join rested in me and Alissa, and no one else.

After all of our conversations and research and soul searching, Alissa finally let me know where she stood.

"I've decided that I am not going to join. Not because I don't feel that it is right. But this has been your burden for so many years. You have taken it up as your cause and carried it valiantly for all of us. Safe and Sound is my cause and I don't want to do anything to distract me from that."

I knew that with all my heart. Wherever she went, she was advocating for prevention and safety for other parents and their children. She was saving lives.

I tried to blink back tears until I saw that her eyes were equally wet. I let them linger as she continued, "I've watched what that burden has done to you. I see the struggle and the effects that weight has had on you. This is, and has been, your fight. So the decision is entirely yours. Do whatever you need to do. Just know that no matter what, you have all the love and support from us you'll ever need to get you through."

I felt her words reverberate through me. Alissa's selfless decision left me feeling her love and support. I would need to stand alone, but I was not abandoned. I had to find the truth on my own. This was a precious gift only Alissa could provide . . . and was for me to accept.

But still, I wasn't ready to make a decision.

In the months that followed the Pettys' call, I had grown significantly. I was surprised to realize I was able to actually *feel* the raw anger I saw in Monica that night in the NICU after her aunt regurgitated Sandy Hook conspiracies. I was able to recognize the shock and disbelief on the faces of the leaders at Art with Heart after being accosted on the street. I even experienced the hurt and disappointment specifically reserved for myself that, despite everything, I didn't protect Emilie's name or memory like I had wanted to. Living all these experiences and attaching the proper emotions to them with fresh eyes and years of accumulated understanding put the pieces together, helping me see a bigger picture.

Without my walls of protection up to save me, these memories stabbed me deeper than I realized was possible. For days I could hardly breathe, unable to escape a single ounce of pain or shame as I processed each memory and emotion that I had kept at bay through my numbness. I finally got to where the anxiety and pain was manageable, which added more clarity. I grew the ability to more sharply see myself in the world and within my relationships. Every time I retreated inward took me away from someone or something I cared about. Through my anger, lies, and coping, there was distance between me, Alissa, and our girls. I was disengaged from activities like cooking, fishing, and writing that I used to connect with myself and others. In over five years I had gotten to know plenty of acquaintances, but I had not made a new friend since Emilie died.

During this process, my family took a weekend trip to the Oregon coast. We had spent months in another life, during my clinical rotations, living and working on the coast. It was a place we were especially fond of, a place connected to Emilie and our lives before they were infiltrated with grief and conspiracies.

The streets, beaches, and shops were all congested with tourists oblivious to the fact that locals put up with them the same way one accepts nasal congestion when fighting a cold. A nuisance, but also a natural part of life vital to the economy. So, for a few months every year, anyone with a permanent address there adjusts to the invaders, breathing through their mouths to get by.

Despite the crowds, we enjoyed the cool coastal air, felt the nostalgia of a simpler time, and visited the outlet mall to save on back-to-school clothes. Madeline and Samantha, now ages ten and nine, couldn't agree on what clothing stores we should all go to first. We split our foursome into twosomes, and off we went. Madeline and I stopped into stores where I enjoyed how she coordinated new outfits that welcomed her expression and creativity. I marveled at how much she had grown and matured since we first arrived back in the Northwest.

While I pretended to look at shirts for myself, I sensed a familiar but eerie feeling hovering near me. My muscles tensed and coiled. A thin layer of sweat coated the palms of my hands. Instinctively, I moved closer to Madeline without a conscious thought. My eyes were scanning the store for danger when I saw a man staring directly at me. My heart jolted. Quickly, I wrapped an arm around Madeline's shoulders, nudging her to my protective side. I put myself between this man and my daughter, just as I had done in the elevator two years earlier in Seattle.

My eyes continued darting around the store, my brain taking immediate inventory of exits and everyone around us—the mother and daughter to our right, checking price tags, a dad to my left, feeding treats to his baby in a stroller, and the line of customers waiting for the cashier. No more than two or three seconds passed assessing the threat when I glanced back toward the man. He was still staring at me. Then suddenly he smiled.

The smile shook me a bit, catching me off guard, until the woman to Madeline's right spoke up. "Jeffrey, there you are. Come here and look at this shirt."

The man I thought was staring replaced the shirt he was holding back on the rack, walked around the two clothes racks next to me, and joined his wife and daughter. "Oh, I like that!" He beamed at his daughter who appeared to be just younger than Samantha. "Of course you can get it; is there anything else in here you want?"

Madeline, seemingly unaware that anything transpired around us, looked up from the rack in front of her and shrugged noncommittally. "Are you ready to go?" she asked me.

Nobody else in that whole store knew what had transpired in the span of ten seconds, but I was embarrassed and angry. Jeffrey posed no threat to me or Madeline. He was a dad on a shopping trip, just like I was. As we left the store, I wanted to laugh it off—but couldn't. I beat myself up for overreacting. I didn't want to respond like that—I didn't even really choose to; it just happened.

The tension in my jaw was still apparent as we walked down the lane to another store. I detested the idea that I wasn't in complete control of how I reacted when I felt any kind of threat. And I hated even more knowing the what, why, and where it all came from. I still did not want to accept that people like Alex Jones, Wolfgang

Halbig, and their followers had any impact on me. Questions raced through my head all day. How many times had this happened over the years and I didn't even realize it? Did it matter? Just because that man wasn't a threat didn't mean everyone here wasn't, but then, would I ever feel safe again? It was all getting harder and harder to ignore.

A WEEK AFTER OUR TRIP TO THE COAST, we all spent a busy afternoon grocery shopping, getting gas, running errands, and everything else kids can't stand doing with their parents. But our girls were troopers. As I drove past the Wendy's restaurant after leaving Costco, I unexpectedly swerved across two lanes of traffic and made as dramatic a turn as a minivan can make into the parking lot. Everyone seemed shocked until I said, "Do you girls want a frosty?" then whispered to Alissa, "They've been great today; they deserve it." The smiles, giggles, and dramatic entrance had everyone feeling good.

After we parked, everyone started to get out of the minivan—all except for Madeline. I was already standing outside the driver's-side door when I noticed Madeline was still seated with her seat belt on. "What's up?" I asked. "Are you going to come inside?"

Madeline just shook her head "no" and stonily pointed to the car next to us. Something was wrong.

I sat back down in the driver's seat for a moment, while Alissa paused her exit from the passenger's side. "What's going on, Madeline? Are you okay?"

Madeline pointed again to the small beat-up sedan next to us. "That car has an *Infowars* bumper sticker on it. Isn't *Infowars* the same guy that bullies you?"

I gulped. Alissa and I looked at each other for a moment, our eyes reminding us to always answer our children's questions honestly.

"Are you talking about that Alex Jones guy?" I asked, wanting to make sure I was answering the actual question she was asking.

"Yes, *him*, the guy that tells people Emilie didn't die and says mean things about you."

"Uh, you're right, Madeline, *Infowars* is Alex Jones's website."

"Well, I don't want to go inside if someone is going to recognize you." Her voice became suddenly emotional. "I don't want to see someone bully you."

Alissa jumped in. "That's okay, honey. Would you rather we go through the drive-thru instead?"

Just then, two twentysomething men, with gnarly hair, cutoff sleeveless T-shirts, carrying their fast food and sodas, walked past Madeline's closed door. Their car eventually sputtered to life after some encouragement. Music blaring, they drove off.

"Madeline," I began after a moment's pause, "that was a very good observation you made. You are always so sharp at noticing things I don't see all the time. I'm really touched how much you care about me and your family."

Madeline took a deep breath, but the emotion remained on her face.

"Those people are gone now. Would you like to go inside, go through the drive-thru, or just go home?"

Madeline looked at Samantha and inquired, "Do you still want a frosty, Sam?" After receiving a robust confirmation, she said, "Then we can go inside."

I held Madeline's hand walking across the parking lot. It felt tense. Sitting in a booth with plastic benches and a Formica table, I watched Madeline closely. She nibbled at her frosty slowly, almost defensively. Her eyes darted around the room, as if she was taking inventory of the people around her. Whenever the door opened, she glanced up and assessed anyone entering. Her body looked coiled up, ready to spring if needed.

My heart broke witnessing her this way. *Madeline and Samantha are going to follow our example of how we handle things*, I thought to myself . . . as I broke down inside.

After arriving home, I pulled Alissa into our bedroom and shut the door. "Did you see how Madeline was acting once we got inside Wendy's?" I asked, keeping my voice low.

"Yeah, she seemed really tense—that bumper sticker really affected her."

"I know, it totally did." I looked into her eyes. "Alissa, her body was responding the same way mine does when I feel threatened. Do you realize what that means?" I asked with my own tension rising.

"What?"

"It means everything I've done or am doing to protect her, to protect us, isn't working. She was scared, afraid that I would get bullied. It affected her. Every time something happens to us, I keep retreating more and more. I keep pretending—for them—that I'm not affected and that we are okay." My voice remained soft but strong and steady.

"What are you saying, Robbie?" Alissa's soft blue eyes burrowed deep inside me.

"I'm just *lying* to them. I'm lying to myself. They might not know everything, but they feel what we feel. They know, and they see me pretending. They see the threat and me cowering. I want them to know the truth. I want them to know that I can actually protect them. I want them to know their feelings are as valid as mine. They need to know we love them—and that I'll fight for them. I'm ready."

I sat next to Alissa on the bed while I found Josh Koskoff's number.

"Hey, Josh, this is Robbie Parker . . . I'm all in."

Chapter 10
The Emails

"This is total war!" Alex Jones erupted into the camera, fists raised. "You want it, you got it!" he continued, all while his attorney Norm Pattis sat amicably at his side during the tirade.

For over a year, the lawsuit had quietly sauntered along, dragging through the swamp of court proceedings without much fanfare or stories for reporters to write. We heard literally nothing except periodic updates that not much was happening due to Jones. That all changed in June of 2019 when news outlets across the country ran headlines such as: "Child Porn Found in Documents Alex Jones Sent to Lawyers of Sandy Hook Families," and "Alex Jones Denies Sending Child Porn to Lawyers in Sandy Hook Defamation Suit."

The headlines were all true—although they lacked the full story, as headlines are known to do. For over a year, Jones refused to produce documents the court had ordered as part of the routine discovery process. Jones's defense team had tried to have the lawsuit dismissed by filing motions and arguing that his speech, whether you like it or not, is protected by the First Amendment. Jones and his team still needed to prove their case that his speech was protected under Anti-SLAPP laws (laws that allow defendants to quickly dismiss meritless lawsuits that intimidate free speech protected by the First Amendment).

Thus Judge Barbara N. Bellis allowed a process known as discovery to commence and ordered Jones to produce documents that proved his speech was protected along with certain documents and evidence requested by the plaintiffs. After each side received the ordered evidence through discovery, a court date would be set for oral arguments and Judge Bellis could rule in favor or against Jones's motion to have the entire case dismissed. If Jones never wanted to see a courtroom, he could either do what the judge ordered or try to settle out of court.

Discovery was actually supposed to help Jones prove that his speech was not defamatory—all he had to do was deliver the evidence. Yet, despite excuses made and extensions given, he never handed over any *relevant* data. This caused the judge to strongly warn that non-compliance would accrue serious sanctions. Jones also had no intention of trying to settle this case out of court and handing over any of his money to people like me, who he despises. So why didn't he just comply and hand over the evidence that could exonerate him?

Finally, in the eleventh hour, Jones produced metadata for over fifty-seven thousand emails, specifically regarding Sandy Hook, to the court. It was a thirty-yard effort for a one-hundred-yard order that still lacked critical documents the court deemed necessary. Immediately, though, an outside, third-party, data analysis firm was hired, at the plaintiff's expense, to comb through every email to retrieve any pertinent information. In that search, twelve emails were found to contain child pornography. The firm promptly stopped its analysis and contacted our team at Koskoff, who then instantly contacted the FBI.

The subsequent FBI investigation concluded that the child pornography had been embedded into emails sent to various *Infowars* email accounts, as an act of sabotage. No one at *Infowars*, including

Alex Jones, had ever opened those emails or likely even knew about the child pornography they unknowingly transmitted in official court documents. The FBI even said that Alex Jones was a victim in this matter, as they continued to investigate who actually embedded the illegal content into those emails.

After receiving the FBI report, our attorneys at Koskoff notified Jones's attorney Norm Pattis of their inadvertent transmission of child pornography, along with the FBI's findings. They also told Pattis that since they had done nothing illegal, there would be no mention of this to anyone. And our side kept their word. In fact, not one word or slip of this was divulged to the media—or any of the plaintiffs, for that matter.

Jones was justifiably angry that someone attempted to frame him for possession and transmission of child pornography. However, true to form, he couldn't simply accept the official narrative with the most logical conclusion. Instead, Jones strung out another conspiracy. He invited Pattis to join him in the *Infowars* studio, on Friday, June 14, 2019, for a special broadcast where he was going to set the record straight. Only after this broadcast aired did our legal team notify us what had transpired, so we weren't caught off guard about the upcoming media attention.

Jones was dressed in a black Space Force T-shirt that appeared to have spent too much time in the dryer. He positioned himself at the center of his giant desk in front of a stadium-sized Jumbotron screen behind him, with Pattis positioned to his right. In a subdued and pensive tone, Jones described how he submitted tens of thousands of emails to the court as he was instructed. Later, he found out that twelve of those emails contained child porn. He truthfully told his beloved listeners that he had never opened any emails or attachments that contained child porn.

Suddenly Jones pivoted from pensive to menacing as he speculated how odd it was that *our* legal team knew exactly how to find those twelve emails out of the fifty-seven thousand provided, then run straight to the FBI. He kept showing pictures of our lawyer Chris Mattei and accused the law firm of working with Connecticut's two Democratic senators and the Obama administration. With each word and every sentence, his anger became palpable through the screen.

After successfully priming his audience to feel under threat from their enemies and setting himself up as the victim, Jones transitioned from defense to offense, unleashing a tirade that would have long-lasting personal and legal ramifications. Out of nowhere, Jones offered his audience a $100,000 reward for whoever could link the embedded child porn to our law firm and specifically Chris Mattei, much to the surprise of his attorney Norm Pattis, who sat helpless as Jones's tirade went on.

Jones sat erect and raised his arms with cupped hands to proclaim in a dark voice, "I like women with big giant tits and big asses. I don't like kids, you goddamn rapists, F heads." He then raised his head as though he were receiving divine inspiration. "No, no, wait," he began, then paused for dramatic effect . . . "$1 million . . . $1 million for who sent the child porn!"

Every time Pattis attempted to intervene to protect his client, he was quickly dismissed and seemed to only amplify Jones's behavior. Jones kept showing pictures of Chris on his desk and the Jumbotron screen behind him.

"I'll fucking get you in the end, you fucks! I don't care, you are trying to set me up with child porn. I'm going to get your ass. One million dollars, bitch!" Jones then repeatedly pounded his fist on his desk over Chris Mattei's photograph, demanding he wanted a "head on a pike."

Then somehow Jones became even more unhinged. "Total war! You want it, you got it! I'm not into kids like your Democratic Party, you cocksuckers, so get ready! . . . I literally would never have sex with children. I don't like having sex with children."

Mercifully, the stream cut out for a period of time before coming back live with Jones and Pattis still at the "news" desk. Only after the tirade was over was Pattis able to attempt some level of damage control when he spoke. But it was too late.

Early the next week, lawyers for both sides were in front of the judge for a special hearing. Judge Bellis had already reviewed Jones's broadcast in full. She was listening to arguments regarding if she should sanction Jones in any way she felt necessary, like imposing fines or dismissing his motion to dismiss the case without a hearing since he still had not produced any legitimate evidence. After Jones's show, our legal team at Koskoff informed us and the judge that they had to hire security for the safety of their staff and families. After all, they'd been reviewing what Sandy Hook families had been suffering and knew the possible ramifications of Jones's tirade to their safety.

Mr. Pattis, finally able to speak without interruption from his client, quipped back that, "If the attorney Jones had suggested planted child pornography was intimidated, he should be in a new line of work."

Fortunately, the judge was having none of it. She described Jones's actions as "indefensible," "unconscionable," and "possibly criminal behavior." As a sanction, Jones's motion to dismiss the case was revoked. A trial date was set where the plaintiffs and Jones would have to battle each other face-to-face in court.

When I learned about how Jones responded, what he said and what he did, I was surprised that I was surprised. Once again he demonstrated there are no limits or boundaries in which he was contained. Every example only solidified how dangerous he was, and there was concern, even as the walls closed in around him, how dangerous he would become.

What made me emotional, though, was hearing about our legal team being threatened with a bounty placed on their heads. I ached and worried for them, their spouses and children, all of whom did nothing to deserve this. They were trying to help us. Deep inside, I was weighed down with the festering idea that anyone who crossed my path could be subjected to this level of evil.

For me personally, that first year of litigation after joining the lawsuit was surprisingly quiet. By the time my name was added as a plaintiff, the reports about Sandy Hook families suing Alex Jones had already been written and there was barely a whisper about me joining the team. To my relief, among those individuals who learned of the lawsuits, there was near-unanimous support for us, and I never heard one rebuke saying we were "sue happy."

The biggest tremors that came quickly after the lawsuits were filed were in the form of social media companies. Since most of the general public didn't dabble in conspiracy circles online, it was not common knowledge how complicit social media platforms were in the proliferation of conspiracies, as well as open and underhanded harassment against families of murdered children. To our amazement, once the majority of the public became aware of the connection between online algorithms and our suffering, the social media giants systematically banned Jones from their platforms—a move that confirmed what they always denied: they could hear their bottom lines dropping louder, much louder than the Sandy Hook families' pleas they had ignored for so long.

Only a few months before Alex Jones's journeys into the misunderstandings of possessing child pornography debacle, in April of 2019, I received an interesting question from my attorneys, Josh Koskoff and Matthew Blumenthal. They were curious if I would be open to testifying before the United States Senate about censorship and social media.

Apparently, Senator Ted Cruz, a Republican from Texas, and Senator Mazie Hirono, a Democrat from Hawaii, were going to hold a Subcommittee on the Constitution hearing titled, "Stifling

Free Speech: Technological Censorship and the Public Discourse." Josh and Matthew had been contacted to see if any of the Sandy Hook plaintiffs, based on our prolonged history of pleading with and battling social media companies, would be willing to provide testimony for the committee.

They explained that this was totally voluntary. No expense would be paid for or reimbursed by anyone, and the hearing was in less than three days. My body's initial, fight-or-flight reaction immediately washed over me. It would be an expensive, time-consuming trip with a million valid reasons to say no. And yet, I felt a deep call to participate. Perhaps for the first time, I didn't question or doubt that call. I was learning to listen to this feeling anytime it came up now. This was why I joined the trial in the first place: to make positive change.

In just over twenty-four hours, I scraped up plane fare and booked the cheapest hotel in the sketchiest area of town. I drafted and redrafted the prepared testimony I would present to the Senate panel. Then I packed up an old, rarely worn suit and boarded a red-eye flight to Washington, DC.

By the time my flight landed, I had just a few hours before the hearing was set to start. Fueled with more adrenaline and caffeine than sleep, I changed into my suit and found my way to the Dirksen Senate Office Building where the hearing would take place. I received no coaching from any of my lawyers regarding what I should say or even what to expect. In fact, all of them were still in Connecticut, sending their support. I was there alone with only my testimony and instructions on how to get through security at the Senate Office Building and find Senator Hirono's office.

The hearing room felt like an old tavern with no windows. The dark, wooden panels behind the elevated semicircular platform for the senators, along with the lowly table on the floor where panelists were to provide testimony, was exactly like what I had seen on TV. Albeit this room was smaller and there were just a few reporters.

The hearing itself was organized into two panels. The first panel consisted of representatives from various social media companies. Facebook and Twitter, for example, were represented while the YouTube representative claimed to have a conflict. I was part of the second panel, which consisted of a film director, a professor of sociology, another professor of law, and a representative from an anti-abortion group.

I sat in the gallery during the first panel and watched the hearing quickly grow very contentious. Republican senators felt that these companies overly censored conservative voices and content on their platforms, while conversely, the Democratic side accused the social media giants of not doing *enough* to remove dangerous content. They made the argument that social media protocols and coding enabled the spread of such material.

Tempers flared; words flew. It was a definite battle, though it wasn't clear to me who was winning. During one of the recesses, I noticed the team from Twitter huddled around each other whispering. I tried diligently not to be paranoid, as I had been on the elevator and in the clothing store with Madeline, but I swore they were looking at and even pointing to me.

After a few minutes, my suspicions were confirmed as the representative who had been taking a beating approached me. After introducing himself, he told me, "Mr. Parker, I'm so sorry for your loss and everything you've endured over the last six years. I know that we at Twitter didn't do enough to protect you. We are learning from our past and making changes, though I know for you it might feel too little, too late. Again, I just want to say thank you for being here and we are sorry." He then reached out his hand, which I took, and I thanked him sincerely for his apology, thinking of families like the Pettys who could still hope for and benefit from reasonable change.

After the recess was over and the grueling questioning resumed, the same Twitter representative, after being asked a question specifically about Sandy Hook, answered by saying that he heard a Sandy Hook parent was in the room and made it a point to reach out and speak with him. This left me wondering if his gesture and apology were sincere or just another tactic. I didn't know and even then I didn't care. He was there to represent his company. I was there to represent my family. We both had a job to do.

By the time I was seated at the lowly table in front of the tiny microphone and folded piece of paper with my name printed on it, the hearing room lacked the intense atmosphere from the previous panel. I started my statement feeling uneasy, given the set and setting. It felt as though my voice was unsure what to do, like muscles that have not properly warmed up before a game. However, as I spoke to the truths of what my family had endured as a result of the apathetic attitude from the social media companies, I sat up straight with my head raised looking directly at the Senate panel with a voice that became strong and clear. The social media representatives were no longer present, to no one's surprise. So, I highlighted the facts that these companies only felt pressure to change their tactics *after* our lawsuits were filed and the public became aware of their complacency—which hurt their brand. I ended my statement with my belief that these companies have a duty to moderate hateful and defamatory speech—not to limit, but to protect the First Amendment, in the way I believe it was intended.

My testimony was not replayed on CNN or Fox News that night. In fact, from what I could tell, there was not any publicity at all. No new legislation was drafted and voted upon. But that wasn't the point. It had never been the point. I was there to do what I could to protect my family and others. Providing testimony, at least for me, was a step in the right direction. I didn't overcome all my fears and insecurities in forty-eight hours, but now I knew it was a possibility, one opportunity at a time.

As I flew home, I comforted myself with the knowledge that Madeline and Samantha knew I did something that was hard for me, to protect *them*. That was all that mattered.

LATER THAT YEAR, in the fall of 2019, I was on another airplane heading back East. Alex Jones had appealed the trial judge's sanctions against him when his motion to dismiss the case was revoked. The appeal had quickly worked its way to the Connecticut State Supreme Court, who agreed to hear oral arguments.

I arrived at the predetermined meeting place for the Sandy Hook team, wondering how it would feel to see some of the other parents again, as well as our team of lawyers whom I had not yet personally met. I entered the hotel conference room inconspicuously, not wanting to draw much attention to myself. On the other side of the large table against the floor-to-ceiling windows were all of our attorneys: Josh, Chris, Alinor, and Matt I recognized from Zoom calls, with a few other people I didn't recognize. Off to my right, I heard someone say, "Robbie . . . ?" more like a question than a greeting.

I turned my head. Along another wall next to the large coffee dispensers were Dave and Francine Wheeler, Mark and Jackie Barden, Jennifer Hensel, and Nicole Hockley. I hadn't seen any of them since my family relocated to the Pacific Northwest, and apparently me being there caught them by surprise. I had always felt some level of angst when I was around other Sandy Hook parents. The guilt and shame I felt about the suffering I brought upon my family because of my press conference that first day after Emilie's death was compounded when I thought of what the other surviving families went through. In my mind, I was to blame for it ever becoming a movement at all. The videos I saw of them online during my weekly searches, the letters and other forms of harassment they received, and the fact they couldn't be totally comfortable in their own town meetings due to people like Wolfgang Halbig I felt were all on me.

None of the other families ever said or did anything to confirm this presumption, but I was convinced they believed this was all my fault. After our move, I barely had any contact with any of my fellow plaintiffs aside from a few text messages or Zoom calls with our lawyers. Still, it was wonderful to see them again. It had been a long time since I had felt that level of automatic connection. It was a great reminder just how important this group was to me.

After exchanging hugs and pleasantries with all the family members, I finally was able to shake hands and meet our legal team. It really was an honor to meet them and express my utmost gratitude for all their hard work. Now it was time to get to business.

For the next few hours Josh, the State Supreme Court judges, and Jones's lawyer Norm Pattis battled through an intense volley of interrogations. It was nothing like I had anticipated. But our team was not only prepared, but performed masterfully. Norm Pattis, for all his bravado, was no match for them.

Back in the hotel conference room, we all gathered around to discuss and debrief what had just transpired. The lawyers analyzed everything in minute detail similar to a postgame analysis after a big game. It was fascinating to witness. When the dust and energy from the proceedings settled down, some parents spontaneously and organically began to discuss the torment we had survived over the past decade. Francine Wheeler shared an experience about why this fight meant so much to us all.

Years earlier, she broke out of her isolation and comfort zone to attend a conference for mothers whose children had been killed by gun violence. Francine was in an elevator with another grieving mother when the woman saw Francine's necklace and asked, "Who is this?"

Francine answered that the photo was of her beloved son Ben, who was killed when he was six years old.

"What do you mean?"

Francine explained that she was from Sandy Hook and that Ben died in his school's mass shooting.

"But that's impossible!" the woman claimed. "They said that shooting didn't really happen."

Francine was struck dumb, unable to speak, until she finally reiterated that her "real son," "really died" in the "real shooting at Sandy Hook."

To her dismay, there was no slow processing or acceptance of the information. The other woman remained steadfast. "No, no, no, they said it didn't happen, that it was all fake!" she insisted before exiting the elevator.

"She wasn't crazy," Francine stated. "She just really believed it wasn't real."

Other families reiterated a few of their own stories. Mark Barden, whose son Daniel was killed, talked about how someone mailed a letter to let him and his wife, Jackie, to let them know they had gone and urinated on Daniel's grave and headstone. I shared mine about the man in Seattle. Initially hearing these experiences brought up my long-held shame and guilt, feeling I had somehow forced the jump start of the movement onto all of us.

Then, as the stories continued, I began to appreciate hearing them. For the first time in a long time, I didn't feel alone. I felt a little buoyed up, like Alissa did when she came home from one of her Sandy Hook moms retreats. Shared grief was powerful. It didn't alleviate the shame I carried, but listening to their stories helped me bond and connect. And one thing was abundantly clear: our children's lives and memories were being erased. We had been attacked because of lies and we needed to set the record straight.

Eventually, the Connecticut State Supreme Court upheld Judge Bellis's ruling with a unanimous decision. Jones may have felt he had conquered radio, the internet, and social media. However, in a court of law, where everything truly matters at the end of the day, he was beginning to meet his match.

Chapter 11

Worst Enemy

The text messages came fast and unexpected, all of them saying something like this:

> I just wanted to say that the world is super messed up and I am just thinking about you and your family today.
>
> And I can't believe this shit is still happening in our country.

I knew right away this meant another shooting had taken place and my stomach sank. I hadn't received messages quite so strong ten days prior when an assailant opened fire at a supermarket in Buffalo, New York. That's why I immediately knew *these messages* were in regard to another school shooting.

I felt suddenly suffocated, the seat belt too restrictive. As these texts were pouring in, I was sitting in my car in a parent pickup line, of all places, to get Madeline from middle school. Instinctively, I wanted to go inside and get Madeline from her class myself, even if there was just ten minutes before the bell rang. At this point, it had been over nine years since Emilie was killed. After so many shootings since then, sickeningly, I had become accustomed to the emotional toll I would undertake with this news.

First the flashbacks.

Unbidden, videos played in my mind from December 14, 2012. I heard the phone call alerting me that a shooting had taken place at "a school in Newtown." My stomach tightened, knowing what was coming. My brain would replay all my steps from the time I woke up that day until I finally tucked only two of my three daughters into bed that night. Then my brain would analyze and scrutinize all of those steps over and over again.

All the emotion from that time would course through my body as if it happened yesterday: confusion, disbelief, denial, despair, fury, and especially powerlessness, along with a myriad of feelings I'd never been able to put into words.

Eventually, a new video would begin in my head, and it was always crushing. This time, I'd picture the families being forced to live through what I had already been forced to live. Then relived thousands of times.

I hated having to picture parents racing to the scene. I saw their frantic search for their loved ones as they grappled with intense chaos and fear. I saw them huddling together; some were angry, some were shocked, some holding hands and praying, while others sat silently, all of the confused and intense emotions crossing their faces . . . while they waited and waited. Some witnessed other parents reunited with their children, causing a spark of hope to flicker inside of them. But as the time passed, the reunification moments becoming less frequent, I would see hope fading—which feels like a bitter betrayal to your child. The worst is when the unimaginable, the unthinkable becomes their reality. As I sat there at parent pickup, I couldn't stop those videos from playing. It took a decade of practice to not let it overwhelm and completely cripple me. After all, Madeline had had a big day at school. I needed to be completely present for her when she got in the car.

Glancing at the clock, I knew I had time to call my brother, James. I couldn't bring myself to look up anything online about the shootings, but I had to know some of the basic details. "Please, only tell me the first two headlines you find," I said, trying not to let my voice shake.

"Shooting at an elementary school in Uvalde, Texas," he answered, trying to keep it brief and matter-of-fact for me. "Four children and one teacher reported killed."

I hung up the phone and hoped the fatalities would not increase—but somehow knew they would. That same ugly doubt and intuition from long ago was creeping up in my body. I checked and mentally marked the date.

"March twenty-fourth, 2022," I whispered aloud. "This is now their December fourteenth."

Days later, alone at work, when I could steel myself as much as possible, I looked up information about the shooting. For my own internal process, I needed to learn what had happened at Robb Elementary. Brushing it under the rug never did anything for my psyche or my soul. Still, what I saw drained me of all energy. The similarities between Uvalde and Newtown were nauseating.

Much the same as ten years earlier, someone entered the elementary school—a place filled with innocent children and those dedicated to teaching and caring for them. Just like at Sandy Hook, this person was armed with an easily accessible array of killing power in his possession, similar to a soldier at war. His only intent was to kill as many people as possible, and just like at my daughter Emilie's school, he succeeded—simply because he wanted to. At Sandy Hook, it was the lives of twenty children and six teachers. In Uvalde, nineteen children and two teachers were ruthlessly murdered.

The videos repeating in my mind automatically edited themselves as I learned new details. An empty meeting room was replaced with the civic center where reunification happened. Apparently, DNA samples were collected from family members. I wondered how that affected their emotional dissonance of holding hope while fighting the doubt that plagued them.

As the days passed, I watched the same playbook roll out as Alissa and I experienced, just with different characters and circumstances. Some politicians wanted to fight about gun reform; others said it wasn't the time. Leaving all of us to patiently wait till next time, and play the same game *again*—after what I knew would be more senseless loss of life.

Through the years, I'd felt burdened with the desire to get out and do *something*—but never knew how I could actually help without exposing my family to further danger. Even though it wasn't much help for the Uvalde families, at least this time I knew I was *doing something*. As unwilling experts, we'd come to discover that many of these shooters were fueled by lies and disinformation they consumed online. I was finally fighting the Kraken of propaganda and deceit. And I had to believe that my actions and the actions of other parents were making a small difference. This time Alex Jones changed his tune. He didn't claim it was fake or attack victims' families. However, always needing someone to vilify, he casually and falsely claimed the shooter was transgender.

SIX MONTHS BEFORE THE UVALDE SHOOTING, in November of 2021, I sat for my deposition as part of the lawsuit. Alinor Sterling flew out West to support and counsel me through this experience. I had no clue what to expect. All I knew was that Jones's attorney Norm Pattis would try to get me flustered, to slip up and say something stupid or contradict myself. Alinor prepared me like a good coach: "Remember, you don't have to elaborate or explain anything more than what he asks."

Alinor and I met in a hotel conference room on the day of the deposition. In a barely post-pandemic world, this meeting would be held over videoconference. I was nervous and didn't want to eat or drink anything. She reassured me that I could take a break whenever I wanted, and that, in fact, I had more control in how things played out than he did in that I could control the pace and my demeanor. I did not have to let any of his tricks work on me.

In compliance with all the court's discovery orders, I had submitted all my medical and mental health records for Pattis's review. This meant he'd had time to prepare and question me about things I had only ever shared with my wife and in protected confidence to my health providers over the last ten years.

After first scrutinizing my financial situation, Pattis asked if I was ever paid by any special interest groups, had I ever donated to a political campaign, and how much money my wife made fighting for school safety. Then he pivoted to my own personal history.

"Have you ever sought out counseling?" he drilled, his eyes fixed and voice detached. "What was this counseling for? When was this? Did it relate directly to the loss of your daughter?"

Every question felt like a cast from a fishing pole, constantly trying to get close enough to feel a bite as he continued, "Have you had other traumatic instances in your life?" Upon my answer about childhood sexual abuse, he set the hook and started reeling. He probed into every crevice from that experience he could find, poking and prodding into some of the darkest memories I carried. On that train of questioning, he scoured around my adolescence and teenage years, trolling around for another bite. Plunging into deeper waters, he asked me, "Have the impacts you've felt from your abuse had any impact on your marriage?"

"Yes."

With that answer, he felt another tug, leaned forward toward his computer screen, and looked at me thoughtfully for an uncomfortable amount of time. Then his questions restarted, this time rapid fire.

"What kind of impact?"

"How did that affect your spouse?"

"Explain to me exactly what you did."

"DID YOU AND YOUR WIFE EVER SEPARATE? You did? For how long? And why was that?" For over an hour he poked and prodded and forced me to explain how my unhealthy coping patterns, stemming from abuse, grief, and trauma, created distance between me and Alissa. I wasn't as honest with her as she expected me to be, which I hid and felt tremendous shame about. For a period of time, we decided to separate to work on ourselves.

It wasn't bad enough to probe into my darkest memories, now he was stabbing the most painful things I'd ever done to the ones I'd loved most. It shook me up.

LIKE A GOOD COACH, Alinor called for time-outs, privately reminded me what the game plan was, and assured me that I was doing fine. But the idea that any of this information could be used in open court made me extremely anxious. Even though Alinor objected to the questions, I still had to answer them since a judge wasn't present to rule on an objection.

For eight hours, I was forced to answer questions Pattis asked that had little connection to the case. He was looking to break me. After all, a broken witness might not show up to court at all. If they did, Pattis had weapons in his arsenal to tarnish credibility. When he felt that he had sufficiently worn me down, he finally started asking about Alex Jones. Everything over this entire deposition was to set me up for his last wave of questions. "Has Alex Jones traumatized you?"

"Absolutely."

"Has Alex Jones caused you emotional distress?"

"Most definitely."

With each subsequent answer, I felt my momentum shifting from defense to asserting myself. After all, this was the area of my life I had been forced to wake up, to protect my family, and to do enough deep inner work that I could be in this room right now, facing what I was facing.

Pattis went on to make the point that Alex Jones never wrote me a letter. Alex Jones never sent me messages on social media. Alex Jones didn't kill anyone at Sandy Hook. Alex Jones never abused me. Alex Jones didn't cause me and my wife to become separated for a time. "So how can you decipher between any trauma you claim Alex Jones has done to what you experienced as a child? To what you have done as an adult?"

Jones, I said, had unequivocally added to and compounded the trauma I currently experience. Pattis didn't like my very confident answer. So he reframed the question. But when I didn't reframe my answer, he got frustrated and asked another. When I told him just how easy it was for me to distinguish between emotions surrounding sexual abuse–related trauma compared to what Alex Jones had done, he acted incredulous. When I articulated the different ways grief feels inside as compared to how my body responds to threats being made against me, he claimed I wasn't answering his question. When I told him that my abuser wasn't motivated to sexually abuse me because he believed lies he heard from someone else, he tried to interrupt me. And shortly after that, he concluded the deposition.

The following morning, I wrote an email to my lawyers, which read in part:

> Yesterday was a difficult experience, but more importantly really demonstrated the necessity for me to join and fight in this lawsuit. I still find myself battling my natural tendencies to stand back and act as though I'm not affected by what happened yesterday, which is the same approach I took against these conspiracy trolls for years. Not to mention taking that same stance against other forms of abuse and trauma I've experienced. That mindset of ignoring the impacts these people and events have had on my life, in an effort to not give anyone power over me, in reality only siphoned my own power away from me. My history of silence has only left me to suffer in isolation and disconnected me from myself, which has resulted in severe consequences to me and my family.
>
> So thank you for providing an opportunity for me to use my voice and speak truth to what I have endured. For helping me stand up against someone that needs to be held accountable for their actions. Something I was never able to do toward my childhood abuser and Emilie's murderer. Until recently, I've only battled against myself. But yesterday I stood up, used my voice to fight for me and those I love.

Four months later, in March 2022, Jones was scheduled to give his own deposition with our lawyers. After confirming all logistics, our team traveled to Austin, Texas, from Connecticut for an allowed two-day deposition. That morning, Jones didn't show up. Instead, he decided that broadcasting his show was more important. He used his lawyer to lie to the court that he was sick, even providing a doctor's note to substantiate the claim.

Our lawyers were furious, having spent time and money and traveled away from their families for this deposition all to be stood up at the last minute. The judge called for a hearing, to discuss the matter on the very same day. During the hearing, Chris showed the judge a current live broadcast of *Infowars*, with Alex Jones in all his usual vibrato. He was certainly not looking ill, nor was he under the care of doctors as his attorney had just finished arguing.

Judge Bellis quickly slapped a contempt of court charge on Jones as well as a fine of $25,000 a day for every day that he did not sit for a deposition. And for good measure, she ordered that for wasting the opposing counsel's time and money, he would pay all of their expenses for this fool's errand. She further ordered that Alex Jones needed to travel to Connecticut himself to sit for the deposition.

Every single plaintiff followed every single order from the judge. In addition to turning in all of our ordered documents, we showed up on time for our depositions. Alex Jones, however, made every maneuver imaginable to escape having to face the inevitable. Yet every time, after every trick he tried to pull, things only got worse. He'd faced sanctions and fines and even had a State Supreme Court rule unanimously against him.

Alex Jones may have been one of my worst nightmares, but he was his own worst enemy. Finally, his time ran out.

Chapter 12

Bluff Charge and Bitterness

Jones had two separate trial dates in two different states barreling down on him. In the spring of 2022, just before the first trial in Texas was to commence, Jones claimed that three of his shell companies were in debt and filed for bankruptcy. These companies had no employees, no assets, and only existed on paper. This merely delayed the inevitable and finally there was nothing else he could do to squirrel his way out of a courtroom.

In the four years since both lawsuits were filed, despite having multiple sanctions and fines levied against him by both judges, Jones still never produced many court-ordered documents. His current employees and corporate representatives were not prepared for depositions and were antagonistic and obstinate, to put it mildly. During the deposition of a former accountant, the financial records she produced were vastly different from what Jones turned over to the courts. Jones was caught lying and forging financial data.

In the fall of 2021, after years of fighting Jones to comply with the most basic of court rules and decorums, the judges in both states issued default judgments against him. Default rulings are a death sentence in civil litigation proceedings; the ruling means that his non-compliance was so egregious and intentional that he was found guilty of all charges by the judges. The trials would still occur, but only to decide the amount of damages Jones would be responsible to pay the plaintiffs in both Texas and Connecticut.

The Texas trial began in the late summer of 2022, for Scarlett Lewis and Neil Heslin, the parents of Jesse Lewis, a bright, energetic, and compassionate young boy killed at Sandy Hook. Neil was the father I watched get torn apart when he testified in front of the Connecticut State Assembly on the impacts of gun violence and was featured during the notorious Megyn Kelly interview. Both he and Scarlett, who now runs a non-profit focused on social and emotional healing, testified of the harassment and threats they had endured, culminating with the experience of someone firing shots at their home during the night.

A lot of the facts and aspects of that trial were parallel to ours, so some of us in the Connecticut case followed the proceedings closely. In the Texas trial, Jones appeared to act jovial, submissive, and even docile. He still told anyone with a camera that everything said about him was a lie and the whole thing was a "show trial." But in front of the jury and on the stand, he was subdued. At one point, Jones even tried to apologize and admitted he was wrong about Sandy Hook being a hoax. After his appearances in court, he would go to his studio and bash the judge, the proceedings, and even the victims more. On one occasion he made fun of the way Neil communicates while impersonating and mocking him as "being on the spectrum."

His testimony in court, however, wasn't always docile as Judge Maya Guerra Gamble was forced to reprimand and lecture Jones repeatedly. "It seems absurd to instruct you, again, that you must tell the truth while you testify," the Travis County district court judge lectured Jones at one point. "But here I am. You must tell the truth while you testify. This is not your show. You need to slow down and not take what you see as opportunities to further the message you're wanting to further." Despite his calculated but intermittent approach to appear civil, the jury in Texas awarded Scarlet and Neil almost $50 million.

Roughly six weeks later, on September 13, 2022, our trial in Connecticut was officially brought to order. Our team was ready. From the very first day of the trial everyone—from his loyal followers to the media and all of us parents—wanted to know when Jones would finally take the stand himself. Knowing he would have to promise to tell the truth and nothing but the truth.

Originally scheduled to testify during the first week, he balked and no-showed twice within the first six days of the trial. This left a frustrated and embarrassed Norm Pattis trying to explain to the court, again, where his client was.

When our group of parents walked to court on the Wednesday of the second week, rumors were bouncing around that Alex Jones was back in town. Plans were made on how we were to enter the courthouse so as to limit our team and his from crossing paths. Media crews crowded inside and outside of the courthouse, staking out best spots with as much gusto as normal folks before a Fourth of July parade.

I sensed Jones was near when I noticed some fresh faces scattered throughout the courtroom. These were not the regulars we'd grown accustomed to, day in and day out. The newcomers had a different *feel* about them, constantly craning their necks every time the door opened, plus pointing and whispering to each other. When Alissa and I took our seats, I could hear two men blathering loudly a few rows behind me.

"Look, that's Robbie Parker," one said, in a whisper loud enough that everyone could hear.

"Where?" replied his buddy curiously.

"Right in the front, with the gray shirt."

"That's not Robbie Parker, is it? Holy shit, I think it is!"

I stared straight ahead, holding Alissa's hand, pretending we couldn't hear them. Sitting behind me was Nicole Hockley, who stalwartly slid over on the bench to obstruct their view and block any photos with her head.

A few minutes later, I restrained myself from laughing out loud when the bailiff ordered them to put away their phones.

"You're not allowed to take pictures in the courtroom. You were warned. Now give me your phone and come with me."

"What? Why?" the man protested. "You can't take my private property from me; that is my First Amendment right!" He continued arguing all the way through the doors and into the hallway, his friend following right behind, murmuring something about "being targeted."

Lucky for them, Alex Jones was a no-show, again, which allowed them a second chance to see their hero on another day.

The next morning, day seven of the trial, started the same as before. Rumors spread, the media camped out, and other not-so-professional people were filming our daily walk to the courthouse. I noticed an *Infowars* bumper sticker plastered on a stop sign. Our entire group arrived early. Once inside and seated in the bland courtroom, we chatted casually with the other families. I felt how we were forging real friendships with them while getting to know each other on a more personal basis.

Two minutes before court was to begin, Norm Pattis and his client entered the courtroom. Jones wore a sports jacket over a button-up collared shirt, with the top two buttons flayed open, impossible to stretch around his thick neck. He walked awkwardly, seemingly bowlegged with some sort of gimp, then sat heavily in what had been the perpetually empty chair at the defense table.

I was surprised by how unwell and worn-down he appeared. I started to feel sympathy for the awful physical state he was in when the bailiff's voice boomed through the court. "All rise! The Superior Court of Waterbury, Connecticut, is now in session." On cue, Judge Bellis entered the courtroom cordially but assertively with stacks of papers and folders in her hand, confidently marching up to her perch on the stand with another warm smile and greeting.

"Good morning, Bailiff; good morning, everyone. You may be seated." She organized all her belongings, then peered down at the lawyers' tables.

"Mr. Mattei, are you ready to call your next witness?"

"Yes, your Honor," Chris began with a calm reverence that I imagined warriors save for the moment right before battle. "The plaintiffs call Alex Jones."

Our team were not the only ones who had come prepared. I made sure to sit in the front row, where Jones and I would have a clear view of each other at all times, even with his two bodyguards close by. Immediately one thing became clear: whatever role Jones had tried to play during the Texas trial was nowhere to be found in Connecticut. Immediately after being sworn in, Jones's contempt and disdain for this process and in particular for Chris Mattei was on full display.

From the very first question, he squinted at Chris, locking eyes in what I could only interpret as an act of intimidation. He steamrolled questions with responses that had nothing to do with what Chris asked. This caused major disruptions in the proceedings, forcing the judge to constantly correct and admonish him for his behavior. Personally, I was glad to see Jones quit the acting and feigned contrition he tried in the first trial. I was glad he was willing to show this jury who he really was.

Between Jones's actions and Pattis's ill-advised objections, it appeared that there was a strategy to get Chris flustered or obstruct his flow. Chris, however, was having none of it. After all, this was his territory. He had built a career inside a courtroom where arguments could be made with facts. Truth could be found, then put on display for everyone to see. Undeterred by any distraction, Chris continued to follow his own plan of attack, laying out our case for the jury. I sat transfixed, watching this tense and surreal scene unfold right in front of us.

I had wanted to see Alex Jones take the stand for so long, to watch him face facts and be forced to acknowledge the truth. I daydreamed how this day might feel and now it was finally here. There was satisfaction that we had finally, after four years of fighting, forced him to face the situation of his own making. I couldn't help it; I smiled when the judge constantly saddled and bridled his antics and kept him in check. After seeing what he did on his show to innocent people, and what he kept trying to do to Chris, it was almost comical to watch him squirm uncomfortably on the stand as he shuffled in his seat, always adjusting his jacket. It was even satisfying to watch Jones give outrageous responses to questions Chris asked that he then easily debunked by a simple piece of evidence.

When Jones said he wasn't sure what his day-to-day sales were, the court was shown text messages from his business manager, with updated sales reports multiple times in a day. The court knew he was very well aware of all sales and spikes and averages. He made Jones answer questions about the supplements he sold such as Super Male Vitality, Brain Force Ultra, and Vaso Beet. When asked if he knew the overhead on a bottle of Vaso Beet, Jones claimed he didn't know. Chris then displayed an exhibit showing they buy the two-ounce bottle of concentrated beet juice for $4 and sell it for $40.

The *New York Times*, in their coverage of the trial, reported more of these occurrences of Jones denying and Chris confirming evidence:

> Mr. Jones said he could not recall accusing parents of "fake crying" before Mr. Mattei played footage of him doing just that and calling the shooting as "phony as a $3 bill."

He also denied knowing Matthew Mills, who interrupted a Super Bowl postgame interview in 2014 and later disrupted a memorial run planned by the family of a Sandy Hook victim. A video was then played of Mr. Jones interviewing Mr. Mills, praising him as a "stand-up guy" and offering to hire him.

When Jones was asked if he knew that within weeks after the Sandy Hook shooting, families were being harassed due to his lies being spread about them, he responded that he didn't know. Chris then produced an email from one Sandy Hook father, pleading with him to stop broadcasting that the shooting was fake because the families were under attack and their physical safety was being threatened.

This pattern of Chris connecting every dot between Jones's actions and every plaintiff's suffering repeated over and over again that day. Still, every time dots were connected, I was caught off guard by how much it *hurt*. This hurt was familiar but a different flavor than I had experienced before. This was different than grief, not from any abuse or from my own weaknesses. It was a transcendent hurt I felt beyond myself and for every Sandy Hook family present. Finally, I looked directly at Jones—really looked at him. I realized that before that day, there had always been a degree or more of separation between me and him. He was always somewhere else, spreading his lies and hatred, his suspicion and mistrust. I had felt the detrimental effects of his actions for a very long time. But why was it hurting so much and so differently now? My heart felt tied up in knots I was not able to loosen.

Next to me, Erica Lafferty was stoic but crying freely. I watched Francine Wheeler bow her head and cover her face with her hands.

I made eye contact with Nicole Hockley and looked at Ian, Jen, Bill, the Soto family, and all the other plaintiffs. Throughout the trial, I'd learned about the horrific effects Jones's actions had on these families that I had grown to love more deeply through this process. I realized there was no longer a separation between us and Alex Jones. Now we were in the same place together, where we could feel all of the callous hatred he disseminated toward us anew.

I never expected Jones to back down, apologize, or show remorse. It was obvious he needed to protect his business and his brand. I knew he was selfish and embodied extremely narcissistic qualities from the psychologists and psychiatrists who studied him. Those qualities were easy to see. I already knew he didn't care one iota for all he had done to us and our families. Yet, regardless of any emotion I had about him over the last decade, I sat there on that hard bench, and realized I still viewed him as a human being. As a human being, I knew he possessed real feelings, had human desires and needs, wanted to be seen and heard, fought his own fears and insecurities. *Just like the rest of us.*

Though it became clear to me that Jones was incapable of seeing any of us in that way. He wasn't just selfish, mean, and apathetic. Everything he did since December 14, 2012, was intentional and calculated toward inflicting as much agony as possible. This was all done with pure malice. Feeling his derision and hatred toward us brought it all to another level of evil. A truly visceral sensation that could only be discerned by physically sharing the same space at the same time with the most odious representation of a human being I had ever come across.

I watched Chris eviscerate Jones on the stand, connecting painful dots for an entire day. It did not feel how I had anticipated. I just wanted to feel vindicated and watch Jones faced with the truth—sweating in front of the jury with nowhere to hide. I did not expect to receive more clarity that opened my senses to how deeply I was connected to Jones's antics. But Chris still wasn't done. Toward the end of the day, Chris picked up the pace with an intense back-and-forth, going at Jones for comments he made on his show that week: "Didn't you say, 'I'm not going to apologize for anything! I'm right ninety-nine percent of the time!'"

"Yes."

Then Chris's next question caught me by surprise.

With a slow, clear, and calm voice, Chris asked, "Mr. Jones, for years, you repeatedly, repeatedly showed slow-motion video of Robbie Parker walking up to a microphone to give a statement the evening after his daughter Emilie was murdered, correct?"

Oh geez. The last thing I wanted at that moment was to experience another round of Jones's scorn specifically for me, but there was nothing I could do but watch and trust what Chris was doing.

"Now the clip you showed was how long?" Chris continued.

"I don't remember."

"You never once showed Robbie's statement that he gave about his daughter, did you?"

"I don't know."

My leg began bouncing while I watched, knowing they were talking about the press conference clip that I'd grown to hate and feel intense shame over.

"Did you ever watch his full statement?"

"I don't remember."

"Well," Chris simply replied, "we are going to watch it now."

This was my worst nightmare, and right in front of the same man who sneered, who pointed fingers, and mocked me countless times and stomped the memory of my beautiful daughter Emilie into dust. Alissa, knowing how I had come to feel about this video, grabbed my hand tight, while sweat escaped from every pore.

The video started and my eyes fixated on Jones, watching me on the screen, until he quickly turned away. He wasn't able to watch anything more than the doctored clip he had manufactured himself. What echoed now in the courtroom were my heartfelt words, how Alissa and I wanted the world to remember our precious Emilie. The message about a beautiful six-year-old girl full of light and love, with the truth of what actually occurred, rang out like a bell. Chris made sure Alex Jones couldn't escape hearing it all as he sat on the stand with a disgusted look on his face.

Right then I was grateful for his disgust. I had granted him room to be human, but now I knew that Jones forfeited any power he ever had over that press conference in my life. And I was right there to reclaim it.

That day in court, Jones proved that he was nothing more than a caged tiger, lashing out at the world because of his own fears and insecurities. He may have had legions of loyal followers and tens of millions of dollars, but he possessed no love in his heart for himself—or for anyone else. He no longer had any power over me, as I recognized with pity that he was just a bitter, angry, scared and lonely, worn-out man.

Chapter 13

Vanquished

The first full day of Alex Jones's testimony ended with fireworks. After being forced to listen to my entire statement and tribute to Emilie, Jones's internal kettle was boiling. Chris dug in and pushed harder: "Robbie Parker is real . . . in fact, he is sitting right here, isn't he . . . and for years you put a target on his back, didn't you?" Chris's raised voice echoed through the courtroom.

Jones attempted to sidestep the question. "I said his name, but I didn't say other people's names because I didn't know who they were."

Chris continued with intensity, "You put a target on his back just like you did every single parent and loved one sitting here, didn't you?"

Jones lashed out at Chris and the exchange erupted quickly. Pattis shouted objections over Jones's booming voice as he started to monologue about Iraqi children being killed while accusing Chris of being an ambulance chaser.

"Is this a struggle session? Are we in China?" Jones shouted over Pattis's pleas to stop. "I've already apologized, and I'm done apologizing! I stand by what I said, and I don't apologize."

Amid the chaos, Chris fired back, "And you're going to do it again, aren't you?"

Finally, Judge Bellis, who couldn't get a word in edgewise over Jones's continuing tirade, was forced to strike her gavel to get Jones to stop. After having already warned Jones at least a dozen times to not speak over his attorney's objections, she admonished him like a parent speaking to a young child. "You are in a court of law; you have to follow the rules. . . . This is not a press conference; this is clearly not your show. . . . You have to respect the process and follow the rules."

With order restored, Chris hammered back at Jones forcefully. "You expect there will be another mass shooting?"

"There probably will be."

"And when there is, you're going to be ready to pounce?" He then showed a survey on *Infowars*'s website asking, "What will be the next false flag event?" With mass shootings as the top selection. Chris continued with disdain in his voice. "You are already priming your audience, after all of this, to suspect the next people, the next Robbie Parker, are actors too?"

"No," Jones answered nonchalantly. "I didn't write that poll, but I think it's a reasonable question."

Chris appeared disgusted and exasperated. "I'm done, your Honor."

THE FOLLOWING MORNING, Chris returned to court, ready for more. Jones, however, cowered back to his private jet and escaped to the comfort of his *Infowars* headquarters outside of Austin, a place where he remained the arbiter of truth, where his voice reigned supreme . . . and accountability was nowhere to be found.

In Jones's absence, bolting to another state, it felt as though the courtroom itself let out a huge sigh of relief. Fresh air and light flooded back into the room where his dense presence earlier seemed to suffocate everything like a black hole. The proceedings themselves were able to get back on track, with truth and testimonies from the plaintiffs.

Previous testimonies from members of the Soto family, Clint Watts, Bill Aldenberg, David Wheeler, and others had already built a foundation of validity that withstood the heavy weight of Jones's conduct. I could see it in the eyes of the jurors. The remaining testimonies would now hopefully counterbalance his lies and hate with honesty and understanding. On deck for upcoming testimonies were both Alissa and myself.

Alissa was not a plaintiff and was not originally slated to be called as a witness. She had never met any of our legal team until a fortuitous meeting early that summer. Guided by the mere randomness of the universe, Chris Mattei's wife grew up just a few minutes from our home in the Pacific Northwest and during his family's annual visit to the in-laws, we'd met up for ice cream. Within minutes, Chris felt Alissa's integrity and compassion and heard her unique perspective about the case. When he asked if she would consider testifying, she resisted. "This is Robbie's fight, not mine," she said, deflecting. Chris was respectful and understanding, but he could not let go of the growing feeling that her perspective could be helpful for the case. When Josh Koskoff met Alissa, three months later on the eve of the trial, he felt the same way as Chris and also asked if she would be willing to testify. This was not something Alissa wanted or sought, though she was every bit as committed and passionate about supporting the case as anyone else. And exactly because of her commitment to her family and the hoped-for repercussions of the case to stop the harassment of victims' families, Alissa took the stand.

It was an unreal experience for me to watch my beautiful wife be sworn in and seated on a witness stand. This time, I wasn't nervous at all. I knew Alissa would provide exactly what Josh and Chris had envisioned, though it was obvious she had some nervous energy of her own. When Josh asked her about how we met and our early dating experiences, I was surprised by how many times she used the word *embarrassing* to describe the fact that we dated while she was in college and I was still in high school and that my teenage body proportions left me looking pretty gangly. Her candor gave the courtroom a chuckle. That honesty and authenticity was what drew Chris and Josh in, and as the questions became more serious, was what spoke to the jury and the rest of the courtroom, including me.

I cried and smiled hearing Alissa reminisce about Emilie and their relationship. It was a sacred and beautiful friendship they shared. My heart pounded, and I was reminded of how lucky I was to witness something so precious. She spoke about Emilie's creative talents and budding, bubbly personality. When Josh asked her where those talents came from, without any hesitation, Alissa pronounced, "Me."

"So, not Robbie?"

"Oh no, not Robbie," Alissa responded with a cheeky grin, and explained how awkwardly I hold my pencil and can't draw a stick figure to save my life. As she spoke, I remembered once when Emilie asked me to draw a giraffe with her. After a few minutes watching me struggle, she lovingly took the pencil from my fingers and said, "Here, Dad, like this . . ."

Josh went on, "So what attributes, if any, did Robbie and Emilie share?"

Alissa responded softly, "Kindness."

The questions continued to flow through Emilie's short but fully lived life and into the heart of why Alissa was called to testify. Not being a plaintiff herself, Alissa was allowed to speak freely about her impressions of what we experienced and how it pertained to me. Having lived these experiences side by side, I felt prepared. I could relive whatever was asked of her, because I already knew what to expect.

With every question she answered and story she told, I found another layer of depth and clarity about our shared experience. When Alissa described what it was like watching the press conference from the church parking lot or how she felt when she saw comments thrown at us calling Emilie a "whore," for the first time, I witnessed these events through her eyes instead of mine. I deeply felt her heart. It transported me into another reality—Alissa's reality.

It got even more real when she described to Josh how anxious she had become watching a metamorphosis occur inside of me. She described how I had become hypervigilant, distrustful, and withdrawn. "There was this intensity about him; he grew so angry and lost his filter," she recalled, "especially at work."

She recapped for the jury the story of the email I received from the CEO of my company regarding his proposed shift alterations. She articulated how she viewed my emotional reaction and the email I wrote in response.

I was proud of what I wrote and how I stood up for myself, until Alissa continued, "He showed me this email he sent to his boss, and I was so anxious because I was scared that at some point he was going to get fired."

A shock of realization rolled through me. With every noble intention I'd had to be there for her and protect my family from being re-victimized from anyone, I'd failed to see my family clearly, and what they were feeling. Alissa was terrified when I sent that email, and I never noticed.

The hardest part of Alissa's testimony came when Josh asked her if she could explain how these ongoing attacks against me had changed me over the years.

She paused thoughtfully. "It has stolen so much of him. He doesn't trust people . . . he is very defensive and doesn't interact or engage with anyone. He's constantly worried about someone encountering us and if anyone looks at us he immediately grabs us and puts us behind him. The most painful thing is how it has changed his view about himself. He carries so much shame and that it is his fault we got attacked and that all the other families got attacked."

Alissa's reality, how she understood things better than I ever did in my own mind, brought me to tears. I hated that even then I was still learning how much these conspiracies and lies about our family impacted all of us.

After Alissa's testimony was finished, Jennifer Hensel and Francine Wheeler grabbed me in the hallway. With sincere concern, they told me to let go and not carry any shame or responsibility anymore—that there never was any thought, ever, about any of this being my fault.

"We are suing the man that holds the most responsibility for what has happened to all of us," one said. "Release your anger onto him." Their hugs and their words were successful in crumbling down the wall I built up over the years between me and everyone else.

A quick ten-minute recess was not nearly enough time for me to reset after Alissa's gut-wrenching testimony. I did my best to change emotional gears and reached into my pocket for a secret weapon. I unrolled a note that Samantha had slipped inside one of my pants pockets before I left for Connecticut, which read:

> You are not just doing this for you, you are doing this for your family and others.
>
> Keep going! You got this!
>
> —Love, Sam

I tucked the note back into my pocket while walking up to take the stand and tried to take in a deep, calming breath. Inside, my body felt like a charcuterie board of emotions, including fear, nervousness, and insecurity, as well as optimistic to finally have a say and eager to get going.

Chris, feeling a lot of emotion from me, asked, "It must be hard to hear Alissa talk about you in a courtroom about very personal matters?"

"Ycah . . . you know, she said the word *embarrassing* a lot when she talked about us dating. I didn't know she felt that way, so that was hard." I chuckled and smiled at the court's response. This was a purposeful act of defiance, not toward Alissa but for me against the defense. I was determined to show up as just me.

I glanced over at the empty chair next to Pattis. Truthfully, I had always envisioned Alex Jones sitting in the courtroom when I testified, playing out like the perfectly written scene from a movie. Now that the time was here, I was glad he was gone. His presence would have only clouded what I was solidly present to accomplish, and I could say precisely what I needed to say without his antics.

In a way, though, Jones was present. During my time on the stand, Chris played a series of broadcasts where Jones talked about me specifically over the years. December 19, 2012; January 2013; June 2013; February 2014 into 2015, 2016, 2018; and so on. After one particular clip where Jones denied Emilie's last moments in life as real, then mocked me and claimed the entire thing was a made-up hoax, Chris let the video continue another minute. Showing how irate Jones was about the conspiracy in one second, then in the next how he calmly segued into promoting Vaso Beet, the two-ounce bottle of concentrated beet juice he peddles with a 1,000 percent profit margin.

Then, it was my turn. I began to tell my story. It was an amazing sensation to hear my voice—my very own voice—express things I had kept locked behind closed doors for too long. Each answer I gave was like a key that opened up another specific door that either let emotions out or allowed me to actually feel them inside of me.

When I told the jury exactly how awful I felt believing that I failed to protect Emilie's memory, a door opened and let out the bitter taste of guilt and false beliefs that I had *any* control over what other people did or said about my precious daughter. After articulating what it was like for me to find Alissa in a coat closet ten minutes before Emilie's viewing, I felt the real shock from that moment swirling inside. I let it be, not having to rush to deflect it for the first time. Never before in my life had I felt a connection like this with my emotions in a way that was actually liberating and comforting.

As the process repeated itself again and again, I was motivated to keep going, to not hold anything back. When Chris asked me to talk about Alissa and my phone call with the Parkland family, it seemed like anyone listening could feel *exactly* how upset and angry I was about what they were experiencing. As I retold the story about the angry and aggressive man in Seattle, I let it all flow out of me, curse words and all. It felt great not caring anymore about how I might feel or how anyone else would feel hearing this story in its purest, most truthful form. Isn't that exactly what we all came here for anyway?

Evidently, Norm Pattis did not. He did not ask me or Alissa any further questions. Admittedly, I was a bit let down to miss my chance for a true face-off with Jones's team, but nothing could have taken away the euphoric feeling I had walking off the stand. I took the long way back to my seat, passing in front of the defense table along the way with my head held high. Throughout this entire process from the years of litigation, my deposition, the courtroom drama, and my testimony, I knew I had accomplished what I set out to do and more.

The conclusion of the trial would soon be in the jury's hands, but at that moment, it seemed more like a formality. The jury could not give me what I had already received. I had reclaimed Emilie's memory. I strengthened bonds and relationships with the other Sandy Hook families that had become priceless to me. I had learned and grown so much as Alissa and I had come to care for them, their living and their dead, as much as we had our own. I told my story. I took back my power and found my voice again.

On Friday October 7, 2022, after four full weeks of testimony, the jury began deliberating everything that was presented. They were to decide exactly how Alex Jones would owe each plaintiff for his defamatory conduct and intentional infliction of emotional distress.

After a long, three-day weekend plus another full day, the jury finally returned with their verdict. The courtroom was again packed to capacity, with photographers and reporters at the edge of their seats. I was anxious to get everything over with while trying hard not to speculate about the outcome. Friends and family were watching the proceedings live across the country as the award for each plaintiff was read out loud.

Bill Aldenberg: $90 million

Jacqueline Barden: $28.8 million

Mark Barden: $57.6 million

Jennifer Hensel: $52 million

Ian Hockley: $81.6 million

Nicole Hockley: $73.6 million

Erica Lafferty: $76 million

William Sherlach: $36 million

Carlee Soto Parisi: $66 million

Donna Soto: $48 million

Jillian Soto Marino: $68.8 million

Matthew Soto: $57.6 million

David Wheeler: $55 million

Francine Wheeler: $54 million

Robbie Parker: $120 million

As the numbers started flowing out, I was shocked. I couldn't contain the relief I felt in the moment as I sobbed into my hands.

A short while later, our entire group was gathered in an empty courtroom to spend our last moments all together, quietly celebrating what we had all accomplished. We knew we'd likely never see any of that money. Jones had already filed bankruptcy for *Infowars* in the face of this. Still, we were proud that, today, this message would ring out across the nation and even around the whole world, that you could not defame a slain child and get away with it, that you could not pilfer harmful, dangerous conspiracies without repercussion. We hoped it sent a message to all the others working to get rich off continued shootings and other disasters—"Don't even think about it!"—and that it built a path for victims to stand up against hateful bullies. Maybe our courage would lend itself to others too.

At one point I had to ask, "Did anybody get the total amount? I was so shocked, I couldn't keep up with the math in my head."

Matthew Blumenthal showed me a sticky note displaying "$965,000,000," which turned out to be the largest defamation verdict in US history.

"Damn," I said, "that's a lot of beet juice."

A STRONG SENSE OF VALIDATION was thick in the air while we hugged and cried with each other. Besides losing our children, it was the hardest thing we'd ever done in our lives—it was for me anyway. After so many years focusing on what I had lost and finding out what I had given up along the way, I finally knew I had taken something back. While out to dinner that night, I saw news clips flash across TV screens sometimes showing different pictures of me and Emilie holding the baseball or just Emilie with her strikingly blue eyes. Gone was the guilt that I failed her. Gone was the shame I carried needlessly for too long. Back was the pride that I was and will always be Emilie's father. I was grateful to be part of a special group of lawyers and families that worked tirelessly to restore truth and restore the legacy of our children, wives, mothers, and the entire Sandy Hook community.

Epilogue

In Alissa's book, *An Unseen Angel*, she describes an encounter between her and Emilie on the morning of December 14, 2012. After I had left for work, they went to Emilie's room where she picked out an all pink outfit for the day, then turned to Alissa. "Mom, I have something to show you." Emilie pointed to an array of painted stenciled flowers on the wall above her bed. "Do you see these two flowers, Mom? One is pink with a black center and the other is black with a pink center. Don't you see it, Mom? There's a connection! If you look around, you will see there are connections everywhere! Isn't it exciting? Everything is connected!"

Alissa smiled and nodded her head, not fully grasping what deeper meaning Emilie was trying to convey in that moment. But Emilie's message, "Don't you see it . . . everything is connected!" has been powerfully important in our family's journey since her death.

In the darkest and most bitter moments of grief, I have heard Emilie's voice; that connection has helped pull me through painful nights. By way of butterflies and annoying songs and countless other ways, Emilie continues to stay connected with those she loves and cherishes to this very day. I don't believe her message was about her or was some visionary foreshadowing for our soon-to-be felt loss. I believe that, really, everything is connected.

Throughout this journey I have connected with wonderful people, shared beautiful experiences, and felt divine emotions. Yet, I have also become connected to a dark and evil side of our world, filled with hurtful people, awful experiences, and grotesque emotions. I have been connected to perfect strangers expressing genuine love as well as others spewing absolute hate. Along the way, connections have brought my family closer together while other connections have tried to tear us apart. In an effort to maintain and protect those connections to Emilie and my family, I became disconnected with myself while giving up my voice and my power along the way.

In a million years I never could have foreseen how the connection between the love I felt when Emilie was born and the horrendous grief I felt from her death would reconnect me to my wounded inner child in desperate need of healing. There was also no way I could have imagined that beautiful girl I held, loved, and laughed with for over six years could ever be connected to someone as awful and despicable as Alex Jones. Or how the kind and caring families of my daughter's classmates would be plagued by their connection to *Infowars* listeners who were determined to desecrate the memories of Sandy Hook victims and wreak havoc on the Newtown community. The connection we formed with the other families was deep. In belonging to a fraternity with the worst initiation process imaginable, we share a bond that few others understand. It's a bond I imagine every parent would happily abandon, but it is one for which I am grateful. When I brought my family to Sandy Hook in early 2012, we planted our small sapling of a family tree in the community with hopes of a bright future. That tree's roots had not grown deep or wide when Emilie was killed, leaving our tree at risk of withering away alone. But the other Sandy Hook families and the Newtown community intertwined their roots with ours giving our sapling enough love and support to weather the storm. Soon afterward, other families and communities impacted by gun violence and mass shootings integrated their roots with ours, providing understanding and experience. In turn, Alissa and I connected with, loved, and supported other families suffering similar fates that came after us. Everyone providing strength and comfort to complete strangers across the country connected by horrific tragedies and senseless loss of life. Now, a sycamore tree representing strength and perseverance is growing its roots in the middle of a memorial dedicated to twenty-six of those victims.

I also never could have fathomed the number of people my daughter would touch through her own brilliant life. Her example and message has given strength to her family and friends when they have needed it most. She has inspired artists to share their amazing talents with others. In a thousand different ways, Emilie's story continues to connect with people—including you.

My story and Alex Jones's story continue to cross paths. By December of 2022, after jury verdicts and punitive damages awarded in both Texas and Connecticut, Jones is responsible to pay nearly $1.5 billion to the families of Sandy Hook victims. He quickly sought protection from the very government he despises by placing both himself and his business in bankruptcy. However, bankruptcy laws provide no solace for debts accrued from "intentional and malicious conduct," making him responsible for the entire amount for the rest of his life. Every effort Jones made to avoid accountability along this path only forced him to receive harsher consequences. A simple admission of misconstruing information with a sincere apology and correction early on would have cost nothing. If done with proper contrition, the flames from his fiery rhetoric could have been stomped out years before they combusted into requiring a lawsuit to extinguish them. Now he stands at the precipice of losing everything he's built. All because he loved the rewards from his lies more than he respected the truth.

As Jones has become trapped by his actions, I have begun to be freed by mine. I continue to learn that reacting to my traumas with fear and silence greatly disconnected me from myself and others, which only compounded my pain and theirs. It was amazing to feel how standing up, speaking out, and sharing my story wasn't as scary as I anticipated, but empowering, eventually culminating in writing this book, forging even more connections than I ever would have expected. The process of this lawsuit or the amount awarded in the verdict did not make all my insecurities, faulty coping mechanisms, or problems automatically disappear. Yet, as I look back at the most turbulent times in my life, I see how the connections forged along the way have helped me through. The obvious connections of love from family, friends, and strangers, to the painfully beautiful lessons from grief, and the unimaginable hate from conspiracists all led me to a crossroads of my past, present, and future. And these converging paths helped me reclaim my power, find my voice, and reconnect me to myself. Now, as I learn how to share my voice, I see how naturally I have fun, use wit, and run toward every challenge and experience life has to offer—good or bad. There will always be a need for healing in my life. Both for myself and those that I love. That is why I'll continue to seek connection through my story and through the story of Emilie's life.

We are here together because that is exactly how stories work. At the very beginning of this book, I said that this story isn't just mine to share. It is for all of us because we have all lived through these tumultuous times together, in our own ways and along our own paths. Those paths may be different but they have also intersected and connected us along the way. Many of our stories are painful and too often we struggle silently to overcome the worst parts of our lives. My story is as unique to me as yours is to you. My experience was filled with specific obstacles and yet it contains emotions that might feel familiar to you. That is the power of stories to connect and bring us together.

As we continue to share our human experiences with one another, may we do so with greater compassion and empathy. Let's challenge our own convictions and rethink our hardened beliefs so the mirage of our differences may disappear, allowing us to see each other more clearly. It is time we start new conversations that move us forward, forging relationships that will bring us together to receive the healing we all so desperately need. I sincerely hope that you, too, can connect with your power and your voice, however that might look for you. So you may fully embrace every joy life has to offer, creating your own connections wherever you can, then share them with everyone you encounter.

Acknowledgments

This book would never have made it to this point from my personal exploration of my grieving process in 2017 without the help of many people. Of course, my wife, Alissa, and surviving daughters, Madeline and Samantha, deserve the utmost recognition for sharing their lives, love, and support as we have traveled this path together. The words required to express my sincere love and appreciation for all of you simply do not exist. I am also thankful for the life Emilie lived and for her continued connection with those of us who felt her love and kindness for the six and a half years of her life and every day since.

My literary agent, Jan Miller, also deserves my sincere appreciation for seeing something in my writing that I was unable to recognize, and she has stuck with me throughout this entire process. Your expertise, along with Ali Kominsky's help, finally brought this project to fruition. A huge thanks to Mark Shriver, who—after reading a few pages of the first draft—facilitated an introduction between me and Jan, and the rest is history.

To Elizabeth Gassman, Keith Wallman, Clara Linhoff, and the rest of the amazing team at Diversion Books, I have felt extremely safe trusting you with my story. The care in your approach and ability to help guide this project from a vision to what we are now presenting to the world is only possible because, from the very beginning, I felt that you cared about this book as much as I do.

Another wonderful person for whom I have tremendous respect is Bridget Cook-Burch. I am so grateful for your writing chops, advice, insights, and—most importantly—your pushing more and more out of me during the writing process. You helped make this book better, and it was a pleasure working with you. This book wouldn't have made it to Bridget, Elizabeth, or Keith without Meg Gibbons. Meg kept a pulse going in this project at a time when it appeared to be flatlining. Thank you for stepping out of your comfort zone to help keep the hope alive. Many thanks are warranted to Elizabeth Williamson for always being willing to read a draft or jump on a call for advice and support, not only for this book, but for many other projects and for life in general.

I most certainly have to express my love and admiration for all of the Sandy Hook Families that were directly impacted on December 14, 2012. Notably, as mentioned within the book, my fellow plaintiffs in the Alex Jones lawsuit. Thank you for giving me the priceless gift of getting to know you all on a personal and authentic level. Also, to the legal team, including Josh Koskoff, Chris Mattei, Alinor Sterling, and Matthew Blumenthal, along with Erin Susko and Pritika Sheshadri, what a pleasure it was to fight this battle and develop fantastic friendships in those trenches together. A tremendous amount of respect is also warranted for Dan Reed, the documentarian and director of *The Truth vs. Alex Jones*. Your care and professionalism were able to capture this story and shine a bright light on it.

A very special thank you to all my colleagues at Oregon Health Science University who traded shifts, provided encouragement, and made it possible for me to travel coast to coast every week between night shifts so I could attend every day of the trial. I am also very grateful to Betty Cottle and Nancy McPherson for providing wonderful feedback and encouragement when this project was in its infancy. To my brother, James, for being a consistent source of support and best friend whose contributions are not well expressed in the book but are felt every day in my life: Thank you.

To the many people who have encountered me during my journey when I was struggling with grief, anger, or deep maladaptive coping behaviors, I offer my sincerest apologies for any pain or suffering I caused from my poor decisions and behavior. I own them, and I am sorry.

Lastly, to all of Emilie's classmates and educators that were senselessly killed, thank you for the lives you lived, the memories you gave us, and your legacies that we will carry on for the rest of our lives.

About the Author

ROBBIE PARKER is the father of Emilie Parker, one of the twenty children who were tragically killed in the Sandy Hook Elementary School shootings on December 14, 2012. He works as a physician assistant in the Neonatal Intensive Care Unit for Oregon Health Science University and has spent his entire professional career supporting child health and safety. He earned his bachelor of science degree at Weber State University and master of science from Pacific University of Oregon.

You can connect with Robbie at robbieparker.net
and info@robbieparket.net.